DAUGHTERS
OF
DOMINION

Karen L. Carpenter

Daughters of Dominion
Copyright @2020 Karen L. Carpenter

ISBN 9798634098203

Contact author at: riverchurchbaltimore@gmail.com

For more information about the author,
visit: www.riverchurchbaltimore.com

Dedication

This book is dedicated to my earthly Dad, McDonald Abraham Jr. Daddy, it is an honor to be called your daughter. Your unfailing love for me and to all 8 kids was a great example of the Father's love for all of His children.

This book is dedicated to my earthly Mom, Luann Abraham. Mommy, you are the epitome of a Proverbs 31 woman, my example of a faithful wife and mom and a beautiful portrait of a Godly woman.

And to God, my heavenly eternal Father, I love You ABBA. My Creator, My Steadfast Hope, You are the One my heart beats for and the Greatest Daddy in all the world. Thank You for making me Your Daughter.

Contents

Introduction.. 7

Chapter 1 From Ashamed to Accepted 9

Chapter 2 Raising the Standard in a World of Chaos.............. 17

Chapter 3 God's Portrait of a Woman Through His Word....... 31

Chapter 4 The Power of the Seed... 53

Chapter 5 The Gift of a Woman: to Her Husband,
         to Her Children, & to Her World.............................. 81

Chapter 6 Becoming a Daughter 109

Chapter 7 God's Covenant... 127

Chapter 8 Take Dominion, Daughter 139

Epilogue 151

Salvation for You & Daily Confessions 157

Introduction

Dear woman of God,

I want you to know that no matter who you are or what you have been through, no matter where you have come from, your life is about to change! This book is written with the intent of helping women around the world and in different walks of life to discover their purpose and to walk in it wholly as a woman of God, created for a beautiful purpose in Him.

You may have a background of being in church or you may not have ever been in a church a day in your life. It doesn't matter. I don't want you to feel judged or worthless or that you are too far from becoming who God wants you to be. We will not attain perfection until we go to heaven. But we can be challenged and motivated to come up higher and to live holy. With God it is not only possible, but it is easy! The Bible says that His yoke is easy and His burden is light (Matthew 11:30). Let God take the load and pressure off of you to be some superhero or figure of perfection that is impossible to attain. He is your Helper and He will help you to achieve exactly what He has called you to. The grace available to you is grace to do only what He has called you to do. I want you to know that we are not in a competition as women, we are not in a comparison rally, and we are not to be jealous of or hurting one another. Focus, focus, and focus again on the woman in the mirror. The woman you look at everyday. Focus on her heart, cleansing and purifying from within. Focus on loving Jesus and loving others. Then, she will become the woman she so deeply desires to be.

Open your heart, open your mind. Position yourself to receive that which the Spirit is saying to you in these pages to come. And know that whatever it is you are lacking or missing to propel you into your destiny, you can find it in God's Word (which you will find all throughout this book).

I truly believe that in this last hour before the return of Jesus that women around the globe are going to rise up and take their rightful places on the earth to help usher in a beautiful and glorious return of the King to His bride, the church of Jesus Christ. There are souls attached to your obedience and they will all be there to join you on that glorious day!

God loves you, He sent His only Son to die for you. If you were the only woman left on this earth, He still would have done it! You are beautiful, you are worthy, and you are enough! God said He knew you before you were in your mother's womb and He called you, even then, and preordained you for this very special and specific moment in time and history.

I pray that as you read this book, your destiny as a woman and as a daughter is unlocked and unfolded on every page. That your spiritual eyes are opened to the truth of God's Word and that you begin to see and hear the voice of God like never before! As you seek God to take your rightful place as a Daughter, may the very miracle you have sought for be on the way to your doorstep now in Jesus' mighty name!!

With Sincere Love & Prayers,

Karen L. Carpenter

Chapter 1

From Ashamed to Accepted

E veryone has a testimony. You are where you are right now and even having your hands on this book because God brought you somewhere. You are still alive. For a very special and divine purpose, for such a time as this. No matter what you have been through or experienced in your life, you have passed the test! And God is giving you a testimony. Many of our testimonies are still being written. The half has yet been told just how vastly God is going to use you in the days and weeks and months to come my dear sister. The Bible says in Revelation 12:11 *"And they overcame him by the blood of the Lamb, and by the word of their testimony; and they loved not their lives unto the death."* Your testimony is documented and first hand experience that God is real and that He does exactly what He says He is going to do. I can tell others that He can set them free, because I too have been set free. I can tell others that God is the Provider because I know him first hand to be my Provider. I can tell others that He is Redeemer because I have experienced Him as Redeemer personally in my own life. Allow me to share my testimony with you.

I was born in Washington DC in 1980. I was the second child out of 8 children that my parents had. We grew up in a little apartment in Riverdale, Maryland until I was 3 years old and then later moved to a larger home in Lanham and then an even larger home in Bowie. By the time I was 10, we were all saved and water baptized as children in our Baptist church. Going to church was a regular part of life. We always were provided for and quite frankly had it very well. We never lacked. My father was a Minister and a Businessman (a Real Estate and Insurance Broker) and my mother was a stay at home wife. She was able to homeschool us from the time I was late into Elementary School and into my Junior year in High School. Then, she went back to work into the school system as a Speech Therapist. Not only had we begged and begged my parents to go to school as we got older, but my dad was faced with a financial hardship in the business and it was a perfect time financially for my mom to go back to work. Going into the public school system at first seemed like a dream come true. Until I began interacting with the other children. I was called all kind of names from "dumb blonde" to "barbie" to "stick." I was the odd ball that came from another planet. Everyone knew that I came from homeschool and that my mom was my teacher. I was ashamed and embarrassed and did everything I could to fit in. I was tall for my age compared to the boys, very thin (5'7 and 90 lbs), and I had colored my hair blonde and colored in a mole above my lip to look like supermodel Cindy Crawford. Her and Tyra Banks were my role models of the day. I had no clue that kids were skipping school, cursing (what was a curse word?), sleeping together (that was only for marriage), and making jokes about the teachers. A lot of the kids, even in 1998 were openly gay and bisexual and I learned things I never knew about.

At 18 years old, I moved out of my parents house with a bisexual guy from high school to live with him and at 19 I ran off to the courthouse and married this man, to make right our sin. My parents were devastated. 3 years later, the marriage ended in divorce, from him coming out of the closet, being found in a relationship with another man and trying to commit suicide in front of me. For 5 years,

> I was empty and working overtime for the devil trying to drink and party away all of my burdens and numb my feelings of rejection and need for acceptance.

I was going after a modeling career, traveling around Baltimore, NY, and Philadelphia with agencies that had booked me from a Regional Model Audition. I realized after losing a contract with Revlon and feeling totally imperfect and flawed, always being stared at and judged on my worth as a model, that I was done with that endeavor. During those 5 years, I also spent them drinking, clubbing, and partying. I was empty and working overtime for the devil trying to drink and party away all of my burdens and numb my feelings of rejection and need for acceptance. I knew God was trying to get my attention and what I was doing was not helping. I hadn't even been to church since I was a teenager. I was out doing my own thing. The feelings of depression would not go away. Abba Father was working to pursue and convict me, even then.

At 22 years old, I went back to my parent's house as a prodigal, in complete shame and disgrace. I felt like I had wasted years of my life chasing after bags with holes in them. Disappointed, rejected, unclean, and unwanted. I decided to enroll back into the University that I dropped out of due to pursuing a modeling career. It was time to get my life in order and to be successful and independent. While at the University, I met a female minister who took me under her wing and began to disciple me and my two girlfriends (who are still great friends of mine today). She invited us to her Baptist Church in Baltimore, and we went and became members and went faithfully for many years. Things began to change when I attended a Women's Conference and heard a message about a Woman at the Well in John Chapter 4. I had never noticed that passage before and I knew that I was that woman. I had been searching for the well of water from this world to satisfy all of my needs and the void that was in my heart.

There was a void of the love of Jesus and true relationship with Him. Religion could not solve my problems

> I had been searching for the well of water from this world to satisfy all of my needs and the void that was in my heart.

and it never did. But intimacy with the Savior could. I needed a drink from the Living Water so that I would never thirst again. I received a taste of that Living Water at that altar, knowing that something was changing on the inside of me. I was prophesied over at that conference that I was called into the ministry. And many other people began to prophesy the same thing over me as time went on. I began getting hungrier for God and for more of Him and grew a strong desire to pursue the call on my life. I took out my belly button ring, stopped drinking wine on the weekends with my girlfriends, quit watching the Tyra Banks Show, and put an end to casual dating. I realized later that I was a lukewarm Christian and didn't even fully know it or understand it at the time. At 28 years old, my oldest sister moved into my home due to a financial hardship with her 2 boys, my precious little nephews. I only had a 1 bedroom apartment but I loved my sister and wanted to make room for family. Early in the mornings, she would wake and be praying in tongues.

> Religion could not solve my problems and it never did. But intimacy with the Savior could.

She would even be coming home from what she called Revival Encounter services and soul winning. I was curious. It wasn't until she showed me a video of services with Pastor Erik Meares and another video of the Great Awakening Tour with Dr. Rodney Howard-Browne, that I knew I had to go to her church! Little did I know that this was the beginning of the best days of the rest of my life!!! It was here at the Encounter Services in Upper Marlboro, MD that I met my husband, Tony Carpenter. Here, I got touched by the fire of God and experienced the baptism of the Holy Spirit. Here, I learned what it meant to be a radical raw believer of Jesus Christ. I learned how to win souls and to take His Word at face value.

One month later, The Washington DC Great Awakening Tour with Drs. Rodney & Adonica Howard-Browne from Tampa,

Florida came to DC to hold a week of Revival Meetings. I was able to attend the meetings after work, go out soul winning on the streets and in nursing homes and in one week prayed with 384 people to accept Jesus into their hearts! This changed my life forever! They gave

> I learned what it meant to be a radical raw believer of Jesus Christ. I learned how to win souls and to take His Word at face value.

me a scholarship to come to River Bible Institute in Tampa, FL and I said yes to the call. I gave a 2 week's notice at my job, left Graduate School (where I had one semester left to get my MBA), and drove down to Tampa in my BMW 330xi with only $3,000, a suitcase, and some boxes. The rest is history! The Bible school was part of a church and an International Ministry. It is here that piece by piece my life came together like a puzzle and everything that was broken was restored and made whole.

I'm here to testify that God took me from ashamed to accepted, from guilty to reinstated, from condemned to confirmed, from burdened to encouraged, from lost to the Cross! God took me from a wandering orphan and made me a Daughter of the King! Isaiah 61:3 says that God will give unto you "beauty for ashes, the oil of joy for mourning, the garment of praise for the spirit of heaviness; that they might be called the trees of righteousness, the planting of the Lord, that he might be glorified." Then in Jeremiah it reads:

> *"Return, O backsliding children, saith Jehovah; for I am a husband unto you: and I will take you one of a city, and two of a family, and I will bring you to Zion. And I will give you shepherds according to my heart, who shall feed you with knowledge and understanding."*

> Jeremiah 3:14-15 ASV

Your testimony.

1. Write down all of the things that once bound you that happened in your past, from the time you were born until now. Though, we never ponder on or give glory to these things, we do this to look back so we never forget what God brought us out from. Oftentimes, we need to remember just how good and how faithful God has been. Though we look at the past, we never stay there. This is a glimpse of your story that I will explain further how God is going to use this.

    _____

    _____

    _____

    _____

    _____

    _____

    _____

    _____

    _____

    _____

    _____

    _____

2. Now, write down your conversion experience of when you came to Christ. Maybe it was at a church service, in your home, or on the streets. Where was it that you decided to give your life, or rededicate your life to Jesus and what caused this? How did it feel to become born again? Write down a description of what happened in your life. What is it that freed you from your past?

_____

_____

_____

_____

_____

_____

_____

_____

_____

_____

_____

_____

_____

_____

3. Lastly, explain what God is doing in your life now and how He is using you. This is the victory and what summarizes your testimony! Share your life scripture that you have held onto. Share your personal encounter with God and what He did for you.

_____

_____

_____

_____

_____

_____

_____

_____

_____

_____

_____

4. Homework: Share your testimony with at least 3 people this week. Find people who are facing something you once overcame and share with them what God did in your life and encourage them that He can do the same for them.

Chapter 2

Raising the Standard in a World of Chaos

We, as believers, are in this world but not of this world. We are only passing through. This world is not our home.

1 John 2:15-17 says:

"Love not the world, neither the things that are in the world. If any man love the world, the love of the Father is not in him. For all that is in the world, the lust of the flesh, and the lust of the eyes, and the pride of life, is not of the Father, but is of the world. And the world passeth away, and the lust thereof: but he that doeth the will of God abideth forever."

The things that unbelievers live for are temporary and it can all be taken from them faster than a speeding bullet. My dad always used to tell us, "This world will sift you like wheat!" It can if you let it!

Live for Christ! Stop trying to FIT IN. You were not made to fit in. That's what I was trying to do all through

Don't act how people of this world act, but instead be an imitator of Christ and spread the Gospel so others can make heaven their home also.

high school and it never worked. I was never accepted there and never would have been, because God had separated me from my mother's womb for a special calling and purpose. Don't act how people of this world act, but instead be an imitator of Christ and spread the Gospel so others can make heaven their home also.

2 Corinthians 6:17 says *"Wherefore come out from among them, and be ye separate, saith the LORD, and touch not the unclean thing; and I will receive you."*

Philipians 2:15 reads, *"That ye may be blameless and harmless, the sons of God, without rebuke, in the midst of a crooked and perverse nation, among whom ye shine as lights of the world."*

In Isaiah 59:19 it reads *"So shall they fear the name of the Lord from the west, and his glory from the rising of the sun. When the enemy shall come in like a flood, the Spirit of the Lord shall lift up a standard against him."*

You are the standard that God is lifting up and raising up in this world of chaos!

We also read in Romans 12:1-2 *"I beseech you therefore, brethren, by the mercies of God, that ye present your bodies a living sacrifice, holy, acceptable unto God, which is your reasonable service. And be not conformed to this world: but be ye transformed by the renewing of your mind, that ye may prove what is that good, and acceptable, and perfect, will of God."*

We can only know and prove what the perfect will of God is when we live Holy and set apart for Him.

With an unrenewed mind, one cannot possibly distinguish between right and wrong or what the will of the Lord is. The first thing we are instructed to do to find out the will of the Lord is our reasonable service to present our bodies as a living sacrifice, holy and acceptable to God. We shouldn't be walking around in skin tight leggings with our bottoms sticking out and breasts out for the world to indulge in imaginations. We shouldn't be hanging out drunk at bars, sleeping around, or still dancing in the night clubs. We shouldn't even be gossiping or talking evil about one another, sowing discord and contempt. Jesus went to the cross for our holiness!

This is going to set some women free when I say this: You are worth so much more than your body! You are not a piece of meat. You are a valuable and precious woman and daughter of God and your body is HOLY. If some man is trying to cause you to fornicate you need to FLEE! You deserve a husband and not a boyfriend. Your boyfriend is not going to be motivated to marry you because you sleep with him. He will never commit as long as he is getting all the goods and privileges of a spouse for free!

> You are worth so much more than your body! You are not a piece of meat. You are a valuable and precious woman and daughter of God and your body is HOLY.

1 Corinthians 6:19-20 says *"What? Know ye not that your body is the temple of the Holy Ghost which is in you, which ye have of God, and ye are not your own? For ye are bought with a price: therefore glorify God in your body, and in your spirit, which are God's."*

When we sin against our bodies, we sin against God. The Holy Spirit dwells on the inside of us. We cannot put toxins into a pure stream. Protect your temple and provide a holy atmosphere so the anointing can freely flow out of you and into a crazy world that so desperately needs it.

We face a global crisis in this hour of gender identity. God created 2 genders - man and woman. Genesis 5:1-2 says *"In the day that God created man, in the likeness of God made he him; MALE and FEMALE created he them; and blessed them."* Unfortunately, our society is teaching contrary to this and that a person can be whatever they "feel" like being on any given day.

Even allowing persons to change the gender on their birth certificates. They say men can be women and women can be men and whatever mixture of these people want to identify with. It's a total disrespect and disregard for the Creator, who made them *"fearfully and wonderfully"* (Psalm 139:14) and in His very image. This agenda is even being taught to children in our schools, and outrageous as it sounds, children are getting sex changes based on how they are encouraged to *"feel"*. This is totally contrary to how God has made them.

God created male and female with the purpose of multiplying the earth, to subdue it and take dominion. When man does this, they glorify Him. The enemy is well aware of this and this is why he confused the minds of the people. He created perversion and sexual abuse and a lack of self identity and awareness of who they are in Christ. His whole agenda is to break apart God's order in the family and to cut off God's creation from the eternal Covenant He made with them. Two men cannot reproduce and multiply and neither can two women. It is perversion and wickedness. It is the very reason God sent the flood to the earth to destroy mankind, with the exception of the righteous Noah and his family. Sodom and Gomorrah were wiped off the map due to this immorality.

> His whole agenda is to break apart God's order in the family and to cut off God's creation from the eternal Covenant He made with them.

Unfortunately, as believers are working to populate heaven, the devil is working to populate hell. We can see his agenda in John 10:10: *"The thief cometh not, but for to steal, kill, and to destroy: I am come that they might have life, and that they might have it more abundantly."* The devil's plan is to steal your identity in Christ, to kill all hopes of ever being in Him, and to destroy your destiny by keeping you bound to confusion, lust and oppression. The reason so many homosexuals are depressed and suicidal is because they have forced their minds to believe that they were BORN gay. This is a lie from the devil and this is why the Bible says a man must be born AGAIN. We are born into sin and that's why we have to make our own decision to be born again. You don't have to wait until you are perfect or you are strong enough to stop sinning to give your life to Jesus. It is when you give your life to Jesus that He helps you to overcome sin and to live a life of victory.

The new birth makes you completely new. It's the miracle of being born again and it truly is supernatural. When you become born again, you know it! Everything starts to make sense! The trees are greener, the sky is bluer, your eyes are opened and heaven is so real to you. Let me ask you a question. When a baby is born, does that baby have a past? Is that baby struggling with sexual sin or a drug addiction or lying or stealing? Absolutely not. That sweet little baby has no record of any wrong. That my friend is the beauty of becoming a new creature in Christ and being born again. Heaven wipes away every record of wrong from your past! Hallelujah!

Look at 2 Corinthians 5:17 - *"Therefore if any man be in Christ, he is a new creature: old things are passed away; behold, all things are become new."* I want to encourage you now my sister that if you are unsure whether you are born again, please go to the last section of this book now. I want to pray with you.

Freedom is not coming out of a closet, announcing your hidden sexuality. True freedom is being EXACTLY who God created you to be! Nothing more, nothing less, nothing else. Period. The devil likes secrets and wants you to isolate and feel like you're all alone and that no one understands. However, I'm here to tell you that the Father loves you! And there is freedom and complete liberty in Jesus Christ. You can be free from every curse and bondage of

> True freedom is being EXACTLY who God created you to be!

perversion and lust. If God set me totally free from memories of childhood molestation and exposure to pornography, then He is faithful and true and can and will do the same for you. You don't even have to cut yourself, because He took the cuts in the stripes on His back for all of your sin. The punishment was already taken! Now you can be free! Glory to God!

In this world of chaos, we can raise a standard against sexual exploitation! We are in a world where sex sells. Everywhere you look, you can see women being used and advertised as sexual objects to sell a product, or to sell a service. Pornography, Prostitution, & Sex Trafficking is at an all time high. Women deep down in their hearts do not want to be used as sexual objects for money. Most of these women are modeling nude or half nude or prostituting to financial care for themselves and/or their children. The god of this world (Satan) has blinded them to the evil and demonic spirit of lust behind it all. His reason? To steal, to kill, and to destroy them eternally.

I remember doing Jail ministry while in Florida, and I was privileged to host a ladies water baptism service. 27 women got saved and rededicated their lives to Jesus. As I offered prayer for them when they came out from the water, they were weeping and saying to me that God set them free from prostitution and they didn't want to sell their bodies or do drugs anymore. One woman shared with me that she was prostituting to take care of her children, but now God has given them a new mom!

> In a world of chaos, we can be the standard to break the rock into pieces!

Ladies, we are to be the salt and the light. In a world of chaos, we can be the standard to break the rock into pieces! The hammer to shatter every plan of the enemy and the woman God uses to break yokes and sets the captive free! You are a PACESETTER! And you will not conform!

Look at Matthew 5:13-16 *"Ye are the salt of the earth: but if the salt have lost his savor, wherewith shall it be salted? It is thenceforth good for nothing, but to be cast out, and to be trodden under foot of men. Ye are the light of the world, A city that is set on a hill cannot be hid. Neither do men light a candle, and put it under a bushel, but on a candlestick; and it giveth light unto all that are in the house. Let your light so shine before men, that they may see your good works, and glorify your Father which is in heaven."*

The woman at the well in John Chapter 4 had one encounter with Jesus, the Living Water. And when she did, the Bible says she dropped her waterpot (that which sustained her physically) and began to blaze abroad this man, this Prophet, the Messiah, that told her everything about herself and offered Living Water to drink. You can be a witness of the goodness of God through the testimony that Jesus is giving you even right now!!

Let's take a peek at the very beginning and what God established for woman:

Genesis 1:26-28

"And God said, Let us make man in our image, after our likeness: and let them have dominion over the fish of the sea, and over the fowl of the air, and over the cattle, and over all the earth, and over every creeping thing that creepeth upon the earth."

So God created man in his own image, in the image of God created he him; male and female created he them.

And God blessed them, and God said unto them, Be fruitful, and multiply, and replenish the earth, and subdue it: and have dominion over the fish of the sea, and over the fowl of the air, and over every living thing that moveth upon the earth.

When God created man, he created them equal and in the image of God. When God said "Let us make man in our image".

He was saying, Let us, the Father, Son & Holy Spirit, make male and female in our very image and after our very own likeness.

He then says that He created male AND female. And God blessed THEM and told them BOTH to "Be fruitful, multiply, and replenish the earth." The LORD said and is still saying "TAKE DOMINION DAUGHTER!" God says to take your rightful place in this world of chaos and bring My God-divine order and mandate to fruition. Dominate this world with the love of Jesus and His perfect will for all of creation. THRIVE! And glorify me with all you do!

> Dominate this world with the love of Jesus and His perfect will for all of creation.

God's perfect plan was for male and female to work together and take dominion and subdue the earth. Woman was taken out of the side of the man, from his rib as equal with him. She was not taken out of his head to rule and dominate over him and she was not taken from under his feet to be trampled upon. Adam was to cover his wife and to protect her and provide for her: spiritually, mentally, physically, and emotionally. When Adam failed to cover his wife and when she failed to be under the authority, covering and protection of her husband, that's when the devil came and tempted her to eat of the forbidden fruit. Their eyes were opened to good and evil, they discovered they were naked, and God had to put them out of the Garden. The perfect plan God had for man was destroyed.

Failure to comply with the structure set forth in the Bible is an explanation of why we see so much chaos and brokenness in families today. Women are still leading their husband's outside of the will of God, and husbands are still leaving their wives alone to roam and search for answers that she is receiving from the devil - and even other women are being used by the devil!

We even see in the world today that on the account of feminism and women's rights, women are rioting in the streets half naked, some topless, holding up vulgar signage and screaming out curse words. Some women even have the audacity to bring their daughters to these riots. They are angry and pushing an agenda for a woman's right to kill the baby in her womb and for a woman's right to marry another woman. There is a demonic agenda at the core of these protests. It's all a part of the devil's plan to destroy the family that God Himself instituted from the very beginning.

Two women married to each other cannot be fruitful and multiply anything! God created the basis for the family in the first chapter of the first book of His Word. It is not to be compromised by sin and lust and rebellion. They call the agenda in the name of love but it is actually in the name of lust and witchcraft.

You, my sister, are a STANDARD. Not lukewarm, not complacent, not silent, not hiding, but a standard of righteousness and for the Word of God on this earth today. A standard is a level of quality or attainment. The standard is set in God's Word and we are living breathing standards and examples to the lost. How high is your standard for Jesus? How important is His call and Word to you? What have you decided to place over Him? At what level are you willing to break that standard to fit in, be accepted, or to avoid persecution? A world in chaos needs a man or woman of God in position to bring hope! To be the antidote!

> You, my sister, are a STANDARD. Not lukewarm, not complacent, not silent, not hiding, but a standard of righteousness and for the Word of God on this earth today.

The Bible says in 1 Peter 2:9 *"But ye are a chosen generation, a royal priesthood, an holy nation, a peculiar people; that ye should shew forth the praises of him who hath called you out of darkness into his marvellous light."* You are in this world, but not of this world. You are called of God and you hold the keys to the kingdom! You are a blood bought, spirit-filled believer of Jesus Christ! You are seated in heavenly places in Christ Jesus and the devil is under your feet!

Look at Ephesians 6:10-18:

> *Finally, my brethren, be strong in the Lord, and in the power of his might.*
>
> *Put on the whole armour of God, that ye may be able to stand against the wiles of the devil.*
>
> *For we wrestle not against flesh and blood, but against principalities, against powers, against the rulers of the darkness of this world, against spiritual wickedness in high places.*
>
> ***Wherefore take unto you the whole armour of God, that ye may be able to withstand in the evil day, and having done all, to stand.***
>
> ***Stand therefore,*** *having your loins girt about with truth, and having on the breastplate of righteousness;*
>
> *And your feet shod with the preparation of the gospel of peace;*
>
> *Above all, taking the shield of faith, wherewith ye shall be able to quench all the fiery darts of the wicked.*
>
> *And take the helmet of salvation, and the sword of the Spirit, which is the word of God:*
>
> *Praying always with all prayer and supplication in the Spirit, and watching thereunto with all perseverance and supplication for all saints.*

We have to realize what we are up against as the body of Christ. We are at a war with the enemy himself for the souls of mankind and we don't have long until Jesus returns. It is a mandate that we keep ourselves strong and suited up with the whole armour of God. Notice the emphasis on standing. We must stand. In order to stand, we must put on our armour! The root word in standard is "**stand**". That means that we are to be firm, unwavering, solid,

> If we, as believers don't take a stand, then what hope is there for a lost world drowned in chaos and demonic oppression?

and unmovable. If we, as believers don't take a stand, then what hope is there for a lost world drowned in chaos and demonic oppression? Who else is going to bring them hope, freedom and deliverance?

1. What are some things that you recognized, while reading this Chapter, that the Lord is speaking to you about giving up?

   _____

   _____

   _____

   _____

   _____

   _____

   _____

   _____

   _____

   _____

   _____

   _____

   _____

   _____

   _____

   _____

   _____

2. Identify 2 things that we as believers can do to raise a standard in this world?

_____

_____

_____

_____

_____

_____

3. List 3 things that you can do now to raise a standard amongst your peers, coworkers, friends and family members:

a. _____

_____

_____

_____

b. _____

_____

_____

_____

c. _____

_____

_____

_____

Chapter 3

God's Portrait of a Woman Through His Word

So, what does a woman of God, a daughter of the King, look like? We have gotten Jesus in our hearts and ready to be the standard in our world. Now, we have a renewing of the mind that needs to take place. This is why the Bible says that *we are to work out our salvation with fear and trembling* (Philipians 2:12). It takes work to keep your salvation strong and your relationship with Jesus going. Every relationship takes work. Did you have pre-marital counseling with your spouse? That was work you put into and invested into your marriage. In order to keep that marriage, you've got to continue to work at it and invest in it. I would say your salvation and relationship with God is worth working for and maintaining. This is done by meditating on and by keeping God's Word, daily prayer and worship.

Even in my own life, I got saved and it took me many days under the anointing and under the Word of God to learn how to overcome different areas that still needed cleaned up in my life. Only

> Only in the fire of God, and while reading His Word, did things break off of me that no counselor could fix.

in the fire of God, and while reading His Word, did things break off of me that no counselor could fix.

Again, Romans 12:2 reads, *"And be not conformed to this world: but be ye transformed by the **renewing of your mind,** that ye may prove what is that good, and acceptable, and perfect, will of God."*

God's Word is the blueprint for helping us get and keep our lives in divine order and according to His will and purpose. In this Chapter, we are going to look at some key quality traits that God has willed for us, as women of God, to have in our lives.

> God's Word is the blueprint for helping us get and keep our lives in divine order and according to His will and purpose.

The portrait of a Godly woman would consist of the following physical and character traits (in no particular order of importance), according to the Word of God:

Gentle & Quiet spirit

1 Peter 3:1-4

> *"Likewise ye wives, be in subjection to your own husbands; that if any obey not the word, they also may without the word be won by the conversation of the wives. 2 While they behold your chaste conversation coupled with fear. 3 Whose adorning let it not be that outward adorning of the plaiting the hair and the wearing of gold, or of putting on of apparel; 4 But let it be the hidden man of the heart, in that which is not corruptible, even the ornament of a meek and quiet spirit, which is in the sight of God of great price."*

A woman of God is not tempered, lashing out in anger and rage to others. She isn't loud and rambunctious. Gentle means to have a mild, kind, or tender temperament or character. Her volume doesn't have to increase to get people to listen to her in conversation. She also doesn't take advantage of others with her mouth. She is gentle in her demeanor and not aggressive. It is so important for a woman to have class and grace.

> It is so important for a woman to have class and grace.

Notice the Bible says that without word the wives can win their husbands over. A wise woman guards her tongue and does not just ramble off nonsense. On the contrary to a quiet spirit, Proverbs 7:11 *talks about the strange woman and we can see she was far from quiet. "She is loud and stubborn; her feet abide not in her house:"*

I believe quietness starts in the heart. We see in 1 Peter 3 *"a gentle and quiet spirit"*. Your spirit man is the core of who you are and it controls your physical body and actions. You are a 3 part being. You are a spirit, you live in a body and you have a soul (mind, will and emotions). Your spirit can be filled with the Holy Spirit and you can then have the fruit of the Spirit active on the inside of you.

Galatians 5:22 says *"But the fruit of the Spirit is love, joy, peace, long-suffering, gentleness, goodness, faith, meekness, temperance: against such there is no law."* The fruit of the Spirit is in place to bind all the works of the flesh. When you operate in the fruit of the Spirit, you cannot also operate in the works of the flesh. You cannot have the fruit of peace and be laying people out at the same time. You cannot have the fruit of kindness and curse people out. You cannot have the fruit of joy and be angry with everyone who looks at you.

Modest

We can see in Proverbs 7 that the strange woman was wearing the attire of a harlot. Women of God cannot dress like prostitutes.

Life is not a big fashion show where women are walking around showing off immodest clothing, strutting the catwalk. This is a real world, a real battle over good and evil and we are at a real war for the souls of men. As Christian women we have to set and raise the standard in this area. I once heard someone say "Christian women can look good and people just shouldn't be looking." This is very ignorant. If by looking good you have to put on clothing that will show off your body, appear evil, and cause others to stumble, this is an impure motive. Who cares how Hollywood or people around you even dress? What God do you worship? You are a daughter of a Holy God! I tell young ladies, "If what you have on right now, you cannot wear standing at the Judgment Seat of Christ, you need to change clothes!"

> This is a real world, a real battle over good and evil and we are at a real war for the souls of men.

Now ladies, you can dress modestly and still look beautiful. I'm not saying you have to walk around with curtains on or be dressed like a nun or like you walked out of the 1930s. Just cover up your goods and ensure things are not so tight it looks painted on. If you ask the Holy Spirit, He will tell you whether you are modest in your dress.

Dressing modestly doesn't mean you lack confidence. It means that you are so confident in who you are and Whose you are that you don't need to reveal your body to the world to prove it.

Moms, I especially want to encourage you in this area with regards to your daughters. Properly bring them up and allow your daughter to know she is not going to go outside of the house looking like a promiscuous woman. She will not be buying any ungodly clothing. Set the standard, and it starts with you. Encourage them and praise them when they dress modestly. We as adults have all been a teen before and we totally know how it is to want to look good and get attention. There were times as a teenager, I would have on one outfit and once I got around the corner from my parents house, I would take off the long black skirt or baggy dress to reveal the real outfit underneath. Once, I had slipped out of the house in a half top and some skin tight pants when I was about 21 and we ran into our Senior Pastor at a restaurant! Talk about embarrassment. He gave me and my friends a loving reproof. He said "What are y'all wearing? Only your husbands should see you ladies in these clothes." And he was perfectly right. I thought twice again before I went out in public exposing my skin and dressing like a prostitute. My parents raised me better. Sometimes you have to give people a tough word to wake them up to what they can't completely see. They want attention and affirmation but you see that they are a stumbling block to someone's salvation and deliverance.

Let's look at 1 Timothy 2:9 TPT *"And that women would also pray with clean hearts, dressed appropriately and adorned modestly and sensibly, not flaunting their wealth."*

And finally, go to Isaiah 3:16-17 Amplified *"Moreover, the Lord said, "because the daughters of Zion are proud and walk with outstretched necks and seductive (flirtatious, alluring) eyes, and trip along with mincing steps and an affected gait and walk with jingling anklets on their feet, Therefore the Lord will afflict the crown of the head of the daughter of Zion with scabs [making them bald], And the Lord will expose their foreheads (send them into captivity)."*

Keeper of Her Home

Titus 2:3-5 *"The aged women likewise, that they be in behavior as becometh holiness, not false accusers, not given to much wine, teachers of good things; That they may teach the young women to be sober, to love their husbands, to love their children, To be discreet, chaste, KEEPERS AT HOME, good, obedient to their own husbands, that the word of God be not blasphemed."*

Women have been on the go go go and always so busy busy busy. There are times when I have been guilty of the same. But one thing is for sure, we can never ever neglect our homes. A home comes before social activities, church activities, and even being on the phone or internet for hours on end. Our homes should be clean and provide a quiet and restful atmosphere for our husbands and children. Our homes should always be a habitation for the presence of God. Laundry should not be backed up days on end, the place trashed with old food and dishes everywhere and unhealthy meals prepped or no meals prepped for the family, and replaced with fast food every day. It's our job to keep and maintain our homes and the people that are stewarded to us that live in them. Order, proper discipline for the children, family schedules and devotions are key to maintaining a home that is well-kept.

> Our homes should always be a habitation for the presence of God.

We also cannot possibly be a keeper of our home if our very own mouths are destroying everything good that was put into it. Scripture says *"Every wise woman buildeth her house, but the foolish plucketh it down with her own hands."* Proverbs 14:1

This is so profound. Because with the same lips we praise God and turn around and lay into our husbands or get short and nasty with our children. We can see in Proverbs that our mouths have the power to tear down our house or to build it up. A wise woman will choose to build. Do whatever it takes to build your home to what God has designed your home to be for the growth and success of your family in every aspect of life.

We can also look at Proverbs 31:21 - *"She is not afraid of the snow for her household: for all her household are clothed with scarlet."* Her children aren't walking around looking unkept and dirty. Verse 27 says *"She looketh well to the ways of her household, and eateth not the bread of idleness."*

Fears the Lord

Proverbs 31:30 says *"Charm is deceitful, and beauty is vain; but a woman that feareth the Lord, she shall be praised."* When a woman fears God, she has a reverential respect for Him. She would not do anything to disgrace her Lord. She understands His power and authority and position and the effect into her own life. She is open to receive impartation and supernatural strength from the Lord due to her honor and respect for Him. Therefore, she is praised. Not because she is beautiful but because she fears the Lord. Because she fears the Lord she will not neglect her duties at home or commit adultery towards her husband or abandon her children. Her fear of the Lord has positioned her for praise and honor. She stands strong because of this secret. And she holds the Word of God higher than anything else.

Pure & Blameless

Proverbs 31:10 - *"Who can find a virtuous woman? for her price is far above rubies.* Virtuous is having or showing high moral standards. When you are virtuous, the Bible says your worth is far above rubies. So many times, people strive so hard to be worth it and receive the approval and attention of others. It's not by your works or acts or things that you wear to get this affirmation or attention. It's in purity and holiness, walking chaste and blameless in the eyes of GOD. He is the one who approves of you and sets and declares your worth.

Purity is always a matter of the heart. It isn't based on experience, but rather the heart of an individual. Matthew 5:8 says, *"Blessed [are] the pure in heart: for they shall see God."* A pure heart needs to be the cry of our hearts!

Psalm 51:10 says, *"Create in me a clean heart, O God; and renew a right spirit within me."*

This is God's instruction from Peter to the church: Titus 2:3-5 *"The aged women likewise, that they be in behaviour as becometh* holiness, *not false accusers, not given to much wine, teachers of good things; That they may teach the young women to be sober, to love their husbands, to love their children, To be discreet, chaste, keepers at home, good, obedient to their own husbands, that the word of God be not blasphemed."*

Kind

Ephesians 4:32 *"And be ye kind one to another, tender-hearted, forgiving one another, even as God for Christ's sake hath forgiven you."*

Proverbs 31:26 *"She openeth her mouth with wisdom; and in her tongue is the law of kindness."*

Being kind has its benefits! Take a look at Genesis 24:14 - *"And let it come to pass, that the damsel to whom I shall say, Let down thy pitcher, I pray thee, that I may drink; and she shall say, Drink, and I will give thy camels drink also: let the same be she that thou hast appointed for thy servant Isaac; and thereby shall I know that thou hast shewed kindness unto my master."* Rebekah was the woman to come to draw water and she saw the servant and served every camel with water to drink. Her kindness to Isaac's servant opened the door to a prophetic act that positioned her to be a wife to Isaac. She did not know why the servant was there. She was merely just being kind.

We cannot overlook the kindness that Ruth showed to Naomi her mother in law and even to Boaz, her husband to be. Kindness was also demonstrated through Queen Esther in her approach to the King and also in her demeanor and communication to her Uncle Mordecai, which saved her very life!!!

Kindness is more than just a mere act. It's an overflow out of the heart. And it's rooted in love. Love is a fruit of the Spirit, and it is evidence of God's love in us. 1 Corinthians 13:4 *"Charity (love) suffereth long, and is kind; charity envieth not; charity vaunteth not itself, is not puffed up."*

Just as being kind opens the door to your husband to find you, being unkind closes the doors and his eyes are blinded. God is protecting him. If you want to be married to a man of God, or to be used by God in a profound way, you have to get baptized in kindness. It has to take over you and you have to put off: selfishness, anger, contention, and anxiety.

Giving

The portrait of the Godly woman is a giving woman. She is not attached to things. Proverbs 31:20 says, "*She stretcheth out her hand to the poor; yea, she reacheth forth her hands to the needy*".

Proverbs 19:17 "*He that hath pity upon the poor lendeth unto the Lord; and that which he hath given will he pay him again*".

We can see so many examples in the Word of God of women that were givers and women that even gave their last to honor the anointing and the work of the Lord. The harlot Rahab opened her house for the spies of Israel and it saved her whole family from being destroyed. Abigail made room to feed the men of God, King David and his servants and she became the 3rd wife of King David. The Shunamite woman opened her home for the Prophet of God. And also the Queen of Sheba brought gifts for King Solomon. In the Gospels, we see radical giving as the widow places her last 2 mites in the offering in front of Jesus. It's then topped off when Mary anoints the feet of Jesus with very expensive perfume worth a year's salary wages. The disciples rebuke her and say that it was a waste and that the money could have been given to the poor. But in Matthew 26:10-13, Jesus said, "*Why trouble ye the woman? for she hath wrought a good work upon me. For ye have the poor always with you; but me ye have not always.*

*For in that she hath poured this ointment on my body, she did it for my burial. Verily I say unto you, **Wheresoever this gospel shall be preached in the whole world, there shall also this, that this woman hath done, be told for a memorial of her.***"

This woman's giving is not only in the Word of God, but Jesus prophesied what we see today, that everywhere in the whole world the story of this woman, a radical giver, who gave her alabaster box to Jesus is preached about. This ointment prepared him for his burial. What a seed to sow!

Strong

A woman's strength is truly remarkable. No matter what obstacles we have overcome or seen other women overcome, we tend to always come out stronger. No matter the obstacle: single parenting, widowhood, rape, abuse, divorce, miscarriage, or homelessness, women for centuries around the world have relied on the strength of God. They rely on it to not only survive difficult times, but to come out on top. We come out stronger and wiser and more influential to all those around us. Women like my mom, my big sister, grandmother, mother in law, and my Pastor, I sincerely look up to and I marvel at. Because I know that it is only the strength and power of God that kept them and brought them higher in Him.

I love how in Psalm 46:5 it says: *"God is in the midst of her; she shall not be moved; God will help her, and that right early."* Early in the morning, God is her Helper. He is right there with her in the midst of everything. And she cannot be moved. She won't be, she refuses to cave in and fail. 1 Corinthians 15:58 says, *"Therefore, my beloved brethren, be ye stedfast, unmoveable, always abounding in the work of the Lord, forasmuch as ye know that your labour is not in vain in the Lord."* This is so encouraging! That even when it looks like things aren't working out around us, we know beyond a shadow of a doubt that they are! And that our prayers and our work in the spirit is not in vain! A woman that

> A woman that is strong in the Lord refuses to throw in the towel just because of what the natural eye may see.

is strong in the Lord refuses to throw in the towel just because of what the natural eye may see.

Proverbs 31:25 says, *"Strength and honor are her clothing; and she shall rejoice in time to come."* She laughs in the face of destruction and famine. She also knows that *"...the JOY of the Lord is her strength"* (Nehemiah 8:10). She doesn't draw her joy from the things of the world or worthless pleasures, but from the joy of the Holy Spirit. She is clothed in this joy. Joy is a fruit of the spirit and when you allow

> She doesn't draw her joy from the things of the world or worthless pleasures, but from the joy of the Holy Spirit.

Him to fill you with His joy, you can LIVE in that joy! You don't have to be depressed or sad or afraid. You can laugh at the future. Why don't you just go ahead right now and take some Joy! It's free! It is written in Proverbs 30:5 ..."*Weeping may endure for a night, but JOY comes in the morning!"*

Another aspect of a woman's strength is that she is physically strong. Proverbs 31:16-17 says, *"She considereth a field, and buyeth it: with the fruit of her hands she planteth a vineyard. She girdeth her loins with strength, and strengtheneth her arms."* Being fit and strong physically helps you to live longer and to do more, being a bigger blessing to your family and world around you. It also has been medically proven to build endorphins in your body that make you mentally strong and stable.

There is literally a grace that comes on you to be strong. You have to build a backbone in you to endure and to be spiritually strong for the long haul. Apostle Paul says in scripture:

*"But **by the grace of God I am what I am:** and his grace which was bestowed upon me was not in vain; but I laboured more abundantly than they all: yet not I, but the grace of God which was with me."* 1 Corinthians 15:10

The only way to have and keep this strength is by His grace. All you have to do is to ask Him for it and receive it by faith and begin to walk in it, Corresponding actions are always required in your faith.

Ladies, we have to be strong in the Lord and in the power of His might. Not our own might, but in His might.

"Finally, my brethren, be strong in the Lord, and in the power of his might." Ephesians 6:10

"Have I not commanded thee? Be strong and of good courage, be not afraid, neither be thou dismayed; for the Lord thy God is with thee withsoever thou goest." Joshua 1:9

Lastly, I want us to look at Philipians 4:13 *"I can do all things through Christ which strengtheneth me."* Wow! There's NOTHING that we cannot do because HE is the One that is strengthening us! It is His strength, grace and empowerment in us that causes us to prosper. Check out The Passion Translation (TPT) of that same verse: **"And I find that the strength of Christ's explosive power infuses me to conquer every difficulty."** We can count on the strength of God's explosive and dynamite power! For it infuses us to conquer EVERYTHING! It rises us to the top and brings us out of defeat and into victory!

Full of faith

Faith is a belief, a firm persuasion, assurance, firm conviction in something. Faithfulness is the FRUIT of faith. You can be faithful in something you believe in.

Faith is confidence in what we hope for and the assurance that the Lord is working, even though we cannot see it. (Hebrews 11:1) Faith knows that no matter what the situation, in our lives or someone else's that the LORD is working in it. Faith catches it in the spirit realm before it ever manifests in the natural realm. Faith is crazy to those that don't believe or can't understand it. Faith says, "I have it" even when you can't see it.

A great man of God once said, "Faith does not deny the facts. It denies the power of the facts!" Being full of faith means that you are fully persuaded that God is able to do exactly what He said He was going to do and you believe it is already done!

> Being full of faith means that you are fully persuaded that God is able to do exactly what He said He was going to do and you believe it is already done!

The woman full of faith is righteously bold (not domineering) - What she says is taken with respect. However, she isn't masculine in her boldness or using it to stampede on others.

Her faith causes things to happen! We can see in this example that Elizabeth speaking to Mary said, *"And blessed is she that believed: for there shall be a performance of those things which were told her from the Lord."* Luke 1:45 Mary was blessed! Because she believed that the child she carried was to be great! And would save His people from their sins. You can either be full of faith or full of doubt. When you are full of faith, you can see mountains moved.

Mark 11:22-24

And Jesus answering saith unto them, Have faith in God.

For verily I say unto you, That whosoever shall say unto this mountain, Be thou removed, and be thou cast into the sea; and shall not doubt in his heart, but shall believe that those things which he saith shall come to pass; he shall have whatsoever he saith.

Therefore I say unto you, What things soever ye desire, when ye pray, believe that ye receive them, and ye shall have them.

Submissive to Her Own Husband

We are taught multiple times in scripture to submit to our husbands. For example Ephesians 5:22 says, *"Wives, submit yourselves unto your own husbands, as unto the Lord."* and 1 Peter 3:1 reads, *"Likewise, wives, be subject to your own husbands."* According to scripture, the wife does not have authority over her own body, but the husband does (1 Corinthians 7:2-5). It is our duty and privilege to please our husbands! A woman of God pleases her husband and serves him with a glad heart. She trusts him with everything in her because she trusts God in him and God with her. When we honor God and obey His Word, He always honors us!

> When we honor God and obey His Word, He always honors us!

Ephesians 5:33 is an amazing scripture and the Amplified is my favorite version. It really breaks down what it means for a wife to submit to her husband, and it is beautiful.

"However, let each man of you [without exception] love his wife as [being in a sense] his very own self; and let the wife see that she respects and reverences her husband that she notices him, regards him, honors him, prefers him, venerates, and esteems him; and that she defers to him, praises him, and loves and admires him exceedingly]."

Encouraging

She comforts and encourages others. She is not a negative and discouraging woman. When leaving her presence, others feel revitalized, revived, and fulfilled. She encourages others in their God-given tasks and passions and does not cause them to feel ashamed. Her mind is filled with things that are *"true, whatever is honorable, whatever is just, whatever is pure, whatever is lovely, whatever is commendable. (Philipians 4:8)*

When your mind is renewed with the Word of God, only pure streams will come out of you and onto others. A woman can use her influence to be detrimental for the good or for the bad onto others. Especially onto her children and her husband.

For this reason Ephesians 4:29 tells us, *"Let no corrupting talk come out of your mouths, but only such as is good for building up, as fits the occasion, that it may give grace to those who hear".* *Our mouths need to be used to build others according to scripture which says:*

1Thessalonians 5:11 *"Therefore encourage one another and build one another up, just as you are doing".*

Full of wisdom

We read about the wise woman all through Proverbs. Before we end this chapter, let's look at just a few verses of what this Book says about the wise woman.

Proverbs 14:1 *Every wise woman buildeth her house: but the foolish plucketh it down with her hands.*

Proverbs 4:7 **Wisdom is the principal thing;** *therefore get wisdom: and with all thy getting get understanding.*

Psalm 111:10 **The fear of the Lord is the beginning of wisdom:** *a good understanding have all they that do his commandments: his praise endureth for ever.*

Proverbs 10:13 *On the lips of him who has understanding, wisdom is found, but a rod is for the back of him who lacks sense.*

And Proverbs Chapter 8:1-36:

Doth not wisdom cry? and understanding put forth her voice?

She standeth in the top of high places, by the way in the places of the paths.

She crieth at the gates, at the entry of the city, at the coming in at the doors.

Unto you, O men, I call; and my voice is to the sons of man.

O ye simple, understand wisdom: and, ye fools, be ye of an understanding heart.

Hear; for I will speak of excellent things; and the opening of my lips shall be right things.

For my mouth shall speak truth; and wickedness is an abomination to my lips.

All the words of my mouth are in righteousness; there is nothing froward or perverse in them.

They are all plain to him that understandeth, and right to them that find knowledge.

Receive my instruction, and not silver; and knowledge rather than choice gold.

For wisdom is better than rubies; and all the things that may be desired are not to be compared to it.

I wisdom dwell with prudence, and find out knowledge of witty inventions.

The fear of the Lord is to hate evil: pride, and arrogancy, and the evil way, and the froward mouth, do I hate.

Counsel is mine, and sound wisdom: I am understanding; I have strength.

By me kings reign, and princes decree justice.

By me princes rule, and nobles, even all the judges of the earth.

I love them that love me; and those that seek me early shall find me.

Riches and honour are with me; yea, durable riches and righteousness.

My fruit is better than gold, yea, than fine gold; and my revenue than choice silver.

I lead in the way of righteousness, in the midst of the paths of judgment:

That I may cause those that love me to inherit substance; *and I will fill their treasures.*

The Lord possessed me in the beginning of his way, before his works of old.

I was set up from everlasting, from the beginning, or ever the earth was.

When there were no depths, I was brought forth; when there were no fountains abounding with water.

Before the mountains were settled, before the hills was I brought forth:

While as yet he had not made the earth, nor the fields, nor the highest part of the dust of the world.

When he prepared the heavens, I was there: when he set a compass upon the face of the depth:

When he established the clouds above: when he strengthened the fountains of the deep:

When he gave to the sea his decree, that the waters should not pass his commandment: when he appointed the foundations of the earth:

Then I was by him, as one brought up with him: and I was daily his delight, rejoicing always before him;

Rejoicing in the habitable part of his earth; and my delights were with the sons of men.

Now therefore hearken unto me, O ye children: for blessed are they that keep my ways.

Hear instruction, and be wise, and refuse it not.

Blessed is the man that heareth me, watching daily at my gates, waiting at the posts of my doors.

For whoso findeth me findeth life, and shall obtain favour of the Lord.

But he that sinneth against me wrongeth his own soul: all they that hate me love death.

I pray you receive an impartation of the divine wisdom of God today in Jesus' name!!

1. What are some of the character traits that we discussed in God's portrait of a woman, that you personally feel you will improve? And what steps and changes will you make to see them improve?

_____

_____

_____

_____

_____

_____

_____

_____

_____

_____

_____

_____

_____

_____

_____

2. Have you been building your house? What steps can you take to build your house as the wise woman we discussed in the last section?

_____

_____

_____

_____

_____

_____

_____

_____

_____

_____

_____

_____

_____

_____

3. Why is it so important that we have wisdom?

_____

_____

_____

_____

_____

_____

_____

_____

_____

_____

_____

_____

_____

_____

_____

_____

_____

4. List 2 things you can do in each category this week to be a blessing and demonstrate the love of Jesus to others and display the portrait of God's example of a godly woman:

a. Giving _____

_____

_____

_____

b. Kindness_____

_____

_____

_____

c. Encouraging _____

_____

_____

_____

d. Submissive to your own husband _____

_____

_____

_____

_____

_____

Chapter 4

The Power of the Seed

The enemy of our souls has had a plan for the woman's seed from the very beginning. He knew that because of what he did in deceiving man to sin, that a second Adam (Jesus) would have to be sent to redeem mankind back to the Father. And that he would be sentenced to eternal torment. If we take a look back to Genesis, In Chapter 3:15 *"And I will put enmity between thee and the woman, and between thy seed and her seed; it shall bruise thy head, and thou shalt bruise his heel."* The devil knew that his fate was going to be eternal punishment. Ever since then, he was after this Messiah, the Savior of the world.

> The devil knew that his fate was going to be eternal punishment. Ever since then, he was after this Messiah, the Savior of the world.

In all of the many generations of women that led to the birth of Jesus, or were to bear a son of kingdom power, we find that every single one of them were struck with barrenness in an attempt to stop the birth.

1. Sarah, Abraham's first wife (Genesis 11:30, 16:1-2) She was called to be the Mother of Many Nations. And the

devil wanted to block her destiny. He lost! And in her old age, she bore Isaac, the child of promise.

2. Rebekah, Isaac's wife and mother to Jacob (Genesis 25:21)

3. Rachel, one of Jacob's wives (the one whom he loved the most and worked 14 years for, after being tricked into marrying her sister first by her father). Rachel was the mother of Joseph (Genesis 29:31)

4. Manoah's wife (Samson's mother) The devil knew he was in for some trouble with the seed in her womb and Samson took out packs of the wicked army of the Philistines. (Judges 13:2)

5. Hannah, Prophet Samuel's mother (1 Samuel 1:1-5)

6. Ruth - The Bible never said she was barren. But I do want to emphasize that she never conceived a baby with her first husband. And she was married to him for 10 years. The devil took out both the husband of herself and her sister. I believe he saw what was happening in the lineage of Ruth and his plan was to destroy it. When Ruth married Boaz, - the kinsman Redeemer as a type and shadow of Jesus, her womb divinely was opened and she bore Obed. Obed became the father of Jesse and Jesse became the father of David, which goes down to the birth of Jesus Christ, the Messiah.

7. Elizabeth, John the Baptist's mother (Luke 1:7)

Can you see now how the devil has been after the seed of the woman since the very beginning? Now, let's look at just a few examples of how the devil wanted to destroy even babies to stop his fate:

Moses

When Pharaoh saw the children of Israel multiplying and exceedingly mighty and filling the land, he feared them. He commanded the midwives to kill the babies of the Hebrew women when they bore boys, but to save the girls alive. The midwives were unsuccessful, due to the quick labors from the strong Hebrew women.

Exodus 1:16-17

> *And he said, When ye do the office of a midwife to the Hebrew women, and see them upon the stools; if it be a son, then ye shall kill him: but if it be a daughter, then she shall live.*

> *But the midwives feared God, and did not as the king of Egypt commanded them, but saved the men children alive.*

This ladies and gentlemen, is the wicked in command ordering what we perform today - modern day abortions. And they are LEGAL! Full term babies are being murdered, as they are coming out of the womb! This is not about women's rights. This is a WAR and it is between good and evil, righteousness and wickedness. A mass exodus from the enemy to kill the seed of the woman. And we have to draw a line in the sand and say enough is enough.

The Bible says, *"Before I formed thee in the belly I knew thee; and before thou camest forth out of the womb I sanctified thee, and I ordained thee a prophet unto the nations."* Jeremiah 1:5

Every child has a purpose before they were even formed in the belly. And God even says that before the baby Jeremiah came forth out of his mother's womb he was sanctified. The call of God is ordained in a child while in the womb!

If you have ever had an abortion, and you have repented, this is not to make you feel guilty or condemned or ashamed. Your past is covered under the blood of Jesus and you are completely forgiven. He remembers it no more. I am addressing the women, once like myself, who would defend abortion with everything in them just for the sake of defending a political party and to be popular and accepted. I thank God He delivered me from this. You have a Christian mandate and a Constitutional right to speak the truth of God's Word and to shame the devil and plead for righteousness in this land. When God forgives you and heals you for having an abortion, you can be a testimony and you can help other women to make the choice of life and to promote life to others. If you truly love Jesus, stop voting for Pharaoh and allowing wicked men to kill God's precious babies, made in HIS image.

The Bible warns against refusing to call sin just as it is. Isaiah 5:20 says *"Woe unto them that call evil good, and good evil; that put darkness for light, and light for darkness; that put bitter for sweet and sweet for bitter!:"*

The Biblical definition of "woe" is: A condition of deep suffering from misfortune, affliction, or grief. Ruinous trouble: calamity, affliction.

Moving on into the story of Moses, we see that *"Pharaoh charged all his people, saying, Every son that is born ye shall cast into the river, and every daughter ye shall save alive."* Exodus 1:22

Exodus 2:1-10

And there went a man of the house of Levi, and took to wife a daughter of Levi.

And the woman conceived, and bare a son: and when she saw him that he was a goodly child, she hid him three months.

And when she could not longer hide him, she took for him an ark of bulrushes, and daubed it with slime and with pitch, and put the child therein; and she laid it in the flags by the river's brink.

And his sister stood afar off, to wit what would be done to him.

And the daughter of Pharaoh came down to wash herself at the river; and her maidens walked along by the river's side; and when she saw the ark among the flags, she sent her maid to fetch it.

And when she had opened it, she saw the child: and, behold, the babe wept. And she had compassion on him, and said, This is one of the Hebrews' children.

Then said his sister to Pharaoh's daughter, Shall I go and call to thee a nurse of the Hebrew women, that she may nurse the child for thee?

And Pharaoh's daughter said to her, Go. And the maid went and called the child's mother.

And Pharaoh's daughter said unto her, Take this child away, and nurse it for me, and I will give thee thy wages. And the women took the child, and nursed it.

And the child grew, and she brought him unto Pharaoh's daughter, and he became her son. And she called his name Moses: and she said, Because I drew him out of the water.

As we continue to read the book of Exodus, we can see the hand of God in Moses' life and the significance of his birth and the divine protection over him since he was born. Moses freed the children of Israel out of captivity from Egypt through massive signs and wonders, and led them through the wilderness to the border of their future home in Canaan. He received the Ten Commandments from God and delivered them to the people and he also under divine inspiration authored the first 5 books of the Bible. The devil wanted to break the possibility of God's Covenant with Abraham and His people. But this divine plan could not be stopped. The children of Israel had to prevail. Somewhere through the tribe of Judah (one of the 12 tribes of Israel), Jesus would be born through that lineage.

Jesus

The devil from the very beginning has sought after the seed that would bring forth the Messiah. He was trembling at the very thought of his eternal damnation being ratified by this child. There were 14 generations to the birth of Jesus and in the Father's perfect time, the most unlikely woman was chosen on earth to bring forth this chosen Messiah. A virgin. A woman that had never been with a man intimately. It was truly supernatural! The child that was conceived of her was of the Holy Ghost. Prophecy was fulfilled exactly how it was told.

> There were 14 generations to the birth of Jesus and in the Father's perfect time, the most unlikely woman was chosen on earth to bring forth this chosen Messiah.

Matthew 1:18-25

Now the birth of Jesus Christ was on this wise: When as his mother Mary was espoused to Joseph, before they came together, she was found with child of the Holy Ghost.

Then Joseph her husband, being a just man, and not willing to make her a public example, was minded to put her away privily.

But while he thought on these things, behold, the angel of the Lord appeared unto him in a dream, saying, Joseph, thou son of David, fear not to take unto thee Mary thy wife: for that which is conceived in her is of the Holy Ghost.

And she shall bring forth a son, and thou shalt call his name Jesus: for he shall save his people from their sins.

Now all this was done, that it might be fulfilled which was spoken of the Lord by the prophet, saying,

Behold, a virgin shall be with child, and shall bring forth a son, and they shall call his name Emmanuel, which being interpreted is, God with us.

Then Joseph being raised from sleep did as the angel of the Lord had bidden him, and took unto him his wife:

And knew her not till she had brought forth her firstborn son: and he called his name Jesus.

Herod's Wicked Attempt to Kill Jesus

Matthew 2

Now when Jesus was born in Bethlehem of Judaea in the days of Herod the king, behold, there came wise men from the east to Jerusalem,

Saying, Where is he that is born King of the Jews? For we have seen his star in the east, and are come to worship him.

When Herod the king had heard these things, he was troubled, and all Jerusalem with him.

And when he had gathered all the chief priests and scribes of the people together, he demanded of them where Christ should be born.

And they said unto him, In Bethlehem of Judaea: for thus it is written by the prophet,

And thou Bethlehem, in the land of Juda, art not the least among the princes of Juda: for out of thee shall come a Governor, that shall rule my people Israel.

Then Herod, when he had privily called the wise men, enquired of them diligently what time the star appeared.

And he sent them to Bethlehem, and said, Go and search diligently for the young child; and when ye have found him, bring me word again, that I may come and worship him also.

When they had heard the king, they departed; and, lo, the star, which they saw in the east, went before them, till it came and stood over where the young child was.

When they saw the star, they rejoiced with exceeding great joy.

And when they were come into the house, they saw the young child with Mary his mother, and fell down, and worshipped him: and when they had opened their treasures, they presented unto him gifts; gold, and frankincense and myrrh.

And being warned of God in a dream that they should not return to Herod, they departed into their own country another way.

And when they were departed, behold, the angel of the Lord appeareth to Joseph in a dream, saying, Arise, and take the young child and his mother, and flee into Egypt, and be thou there until I bring thee word: for Herod will seek the young child to destroy him.

When he arose, he took the young child and his mother by night, and departed into Egypt:

And was there until the death of Herod: that it might be fulfilled which was spoken of the Lord by the prophet, saying, Out of Egypt have I called my son.

Then Herod, when he saw that he was mocked of the wise men, was exceeding wroth, and sent forth, and slew all the children that were in Bethlehem, and in all the coasts thereof, from two years old and under, according to the time which he had diligently inquired of the wise men.

Then was fulfilled that which was spoken by Jeremiah the prophet, saying,

In Rama was there a voice heard, lamentation, and weeping, and great mourning, Rachel weeping for her children, and would not be comforted, because they are not.

But when Herod was dead, behold, an angel of the Lord appeareth in a dream to Joseph in Egypt,

Saying, Arise, and take the young child and his mother, and go into the land of Israel: for they are dead which sought the young child's life.

And he arose, and took the young child and his mother, and came into the land of Israel.

But when he heard that Archelaus did reign in Judaea in the room of his father Herod, he was afraid to go thither: notwithstanding, being warned of God in a dream, he turned aside into the parts of Galilee:

And he came and dwelt in a city called Nazareth: that it might be fulfilled which was spoken by the prophets, He shall be called a Nazarene.

The devil used Herod in all of his power and authority to attempt at locating Jesus in order to kill him. He was so troubled and angry, he demanded of the wise men to tell him where Christ would be born. This king even lied by telling them that he would come and worship Him. But thank God for dreams!!! God warned the wise men not to go back to Herod. This was divine protection for Jesus and his parents. Joseph then has an encounter with the angel of the Lord, who tells him to depart and flee into Egypt. This messenger speaks to him that Herod is seeking to destroy the child. Herod was so angry that the wise men did not return to tell him where Jesus was, that this wicked man SLEW all of the children that were in Bethlehem at the time from 2 years old and younger. After Herod died, an angel appeared to Joseph again and told him to take the child into Israel and that those that sought the young child's life were now dead. Again, even after this, God warned Joseph in a dream to move again into Galilee, due to Herod's son now reigning there in Egypt. Now, that's supernatural protection!

Before Jesus began His ministry and before any miracles took place, we can see the devil attempted yet again to kill him.

Matthew 4

Then was Jesus led up of the Spirit into the wilderness to be tempted of the devil.

And when he had fasted forty days and forty nights, he was afterward an hungred.

And when the tempter came to him, he said, If thou be the Son of God, command that these stones be made bread.

But he answered and said, It is written, Man shall not live by bread alone, but by every word that proceedeth out of the mouth of God.

Then the devil taketh him up into the holy city, and setteth him on a pinnacle of the temple,

And saith unto him, If thou be the Son of God, cast thyself down: for it is written, He shall give his angels charge concerning thee: and in their hands they shall bear thee up, lest at any time thou dash thy foot against a stone.

Jesus said unto him, It is written again, Thou shalt not tempt the Lord thy God.

Again, the devil taketh him up into an exceeding high mountain, and sheweth him all the kingdoms of the world, and the glory of them;

And saith unto him, All these things will I give thee, if thou wilt fall down and worship me.

Then saith Jesus unto him, Get thee hence, Satan: for it is written, Thou shalt worship the Lord thy God, and him only shalt thou serve.

Then the devil leaveth him, and, behold, angels came and ministered unto him.

Not only did the devil attempt to have Jesus to kill himself. But he also tempted him to give up his call into the ministry. He did not want him to fulfill the purpose of why God sent Him to the earth. The devil figured, if he couldn't take him out as an infant, he will give it another shot when he is an adult and he tried Him when he was at his weakest moment thus far. Jesus had just come off of a 40 day fast and the Bible says he was "hungered". The

TPT (The Passion Translation) says he was "extremely weak and famished". I have fasted for just 7 days and felt weak. See how the enemy tries to attack and stop you when you are at your weakest!

The devil even attempted to kill Jesus when the Jews chased him with stones to kill him and he escaped. Another time, while he was on the boat in the storm and the disciples feared they would all die. Throughout the life of Jesus, God divinely kept Him: to His appointed moment to die on the Cross and to His Resurrection and Ascension.

The power of the seed is substantial. One seed has the power to bring forth miracle fruit and miracle harvest. As Jesus was preparing to go to Calvary, this is what he said:

> The power of the seed is substantial. One seed has the power to bring forth miracle fruit and miracle harvest.

John 12:24 *"Verily, verily, I say unto you, Except a corn of wheat fall into the ground and die, it abideth alone: but if it die, it bringeth forth much fruit."*

A seed by itself is powerless. It stands alone. The power in a seed is in its death. When a seed is planted, it dies, and out of it springs up the harvest. The power of the seed is the power of the seed of Jesus. He is the Incorruptible Seed, the seed that died and resurrected to life! That in His death, He brought eternal life for the harvest of the souls of all humanity. The Bible says clearly He is "the only begotten Son of God". That seed lives in us and we're in that seed. The incorruptible seed doesn't perish, die, pass away or disappear.

We were born again of the Incorruptible seed, the seed of Jesus (who is the Word made flesh) and He abides forever.

1 Peter 1:23

> *"Being born again, not of corruptible seed, but of incorruptible, by the word of God, which liveth and abideth for ever."*

1 Corinthians 15:51-57

> *Behold, I shew you a mystery; We shall not all sleep, but we shall all be changed,*
>
> *In a moment, in the twinkling of an eye, at the last trump: for the trumpet shall sound, and the dead shall be raised incorruptible, and we shall be changed.*
>
> ***For this corruptible must put on incorruption, and this mortal must put on immortality.***
>
> *So when this corruptible shall have put on incorruption, and this mortal shall have put on immortality, then shall be brought to pass the saying that is written, **Death is swallowed up in victory.***
>
> *O death, where is thy sting? O grave, where is thy victory?*
>
> *The sting of death is sin; and the strength of sin is the law.*
>
> *But thanks be to God, which giveth us the victory through our Lord Jesus Christ.*

Because the enemy could not stop the seed of Jesus throughout all the generations of the Old Testament, we have the victory in this world and in all of eternity! Our children have the victory! Death has been swallowed up in victory! We now have power over death because of Jesus! Give Him a shout of praise!!!

The Book of Revelation

We see one final attempt in the Word of God from the enemy to try to take the seed of the woman. Go to Revelation Chapter 12 and let's start in verse 1.

And there appeared a great wonder in heaven; a woman clothed with the sun, and the moon under her feet, and upon her head a crown of twelve stars:

And she being with child cried, travailing in birth, and pained to be delivered.

And there appeared another wonder in heaven; and behold a great red dragon, having seven heads and ten horns, and seven crowns upon his heads.

And his tail drew the third part of the stars of heaven, and did cast them to the earth: and the dragon stood before the woman which was ready to be delivered, for to devour her child as soon as it was born.

And she brought forth a man child, who was to rule all nations with a rod of iron: and her child was caught up unto God, and to his throne.

And the woman fled into the wilderness, where she hath a place prepared of God, that they should feed her there a thousand two hundred and threescore days.

And there was war in heaven: Michael and his angels fought against the dragon; and the dragon fought and his angels,

And prevailed not; neither was their place found any more in heaven.

And the great dragon was cast out, that old serpent, called the Devil, and Satan, which deceiveth the whole world: he was cast out into the earth, and his angels were cast out with him.

And I heard a loud voice saying in heaven, Now is come salvation, and strength, and the kingdom of our God, and the power of his Christ: for the accuser of our brethren is cast down, which accused them before our God day and night.

And they overcame him by the blood of the Lamb, and by the word of their testimony; and they loved not their lives unto the death.

Therefore rejoice, ye heavens, and ye that dwell in them. Woe to the inhabiters of the earth and of the sea! for the devil is come down unto you, having great wrath, because he knoweth that he hath but a short time.

And when the dragon saw that he was cast unto the earth, he persecuted the woman which brought forth the man child.

And to the woman were given two wings of a great eagle, that she might fly into the wilderness, into her place, where she is nourished for a time, and times, and half a time, from the face of the serpent.

And the serpent cast out of his mouth water as a flood after the woman, that he might cause her to be carried away of the flood.

And the earth helped the woman, and the earth opened her mouth, and swallowed up the flood which the dragon cast out of his mouth.

And the dragon was wroth with the woman, and went to make war with the remnant of her seed, which keep the commandments of God, and have the testimony of Jesus Christ.

When Satan discovered that he could not stop the destiny of Jesus, he realized he had to give up on going after the seed. Notice that after Elizabeth (who was pregnant before at the same time as Mary), there are no other barren women mentioned in the New Testament. There was no reason for the devil to shut up any wombs because he had already been defeated and he had already lost the battle. So, here in Revelation 12 we face the times of Apocalypse, the final destruction on the earth. In this chapter, John is sharing his vision of this woman, who was a symbol seen in heaven. She was a sign that God used to reveal something to us through John concerning things that would happen in the end times. Everything here is a sign.

The woman symbolizes Israel. Israel is mentioned often in the Old Testament as a married woman. (Isaiah 54:1-6; Jeremiah 3:1-14; Hosea 2:14-23). Women several times in Revelation represented religious systems. We have:

» Jezebel, associated with a religious system promoting false teaching (Revelation 2:20)

» The Great Harlot, associated with false religion (Revelation 17:2)

» The Bride, associated with the Church (Revelation 19:7-8)

In verse 2 of Revelation 12, we see that this woman is in travail bringing forth a manchild. The manchild represents a company of Jews out of Israel that are saved in the tribulation. The result of the war in heaven will be the casting out of Satan and his angels to the earth.

The first purpose of the dragon (Satan) is going to be to destroy the manchild. This will fail of course, and he will return on the woman who brings forth the manchild and will bitterly persecute her by causing the Antichrist to break his covenant with Israel. (Isaiah 10:20-27; 14:1-27; Jeremiah 30:3-9; Daniel 7:21-27; 8:23-25; 9:27; 11:40-45; Micah 5:3-15).

In verse 14 , the word "might" indicates that those in Israel who are to flee may do so, but not that all will flee into the Wilderness (Petra).

The word "Dragon" is used 13 times and only in Revelation. It is a symbol of Satan, the chief adversary of God.

Generational Seeds

What we see in the book of Genesis is that everything God has created produces after its same kind. Seed will produce after its kind. Fish will produce fish. Cows produce cows. Humans produce humans. This proves that evolution is totally unbiblical. According to the scripture seedtime and harvest applies to every single thing in our lives. This includes generations after their kind. Genesis 8:22 says *"While the earth remaineth, seedtime and harvest, and cold and heat, and summer and winter, and day and night shall not cease."*

The great news is that even though you may have been born into a family of thieves or adulterers, you do still have a choice of whether you will carry on that generational curse or whether you will break it!

Look at Deuteronomy 30:15 & 19:

"See I have set before thee this day life and good, death and evil; I call heaven and earth to record this day against you, that I have set before you life and death, blessing and cursing: therefore choose life, that both thou and thy seed may live."

No matter what kind of family you were brought up in or you currently have, that family does not define you. Nor does it dictate your future. The blood of Jesus cancels out the curse. You are now a new creature in Christ, born again and set apart for the Masters use. You have life and death literally placed before you, You can choose either to have blessings or to have cursings. This demonstrates to us that generational curses are ours only IF we accept them. We have to agree to anything that trespasses in our lives. We also have to determine whether it's in line with or contrary to the Covenant of God established in His written Word for us.

There are no doubt generational curses and witchcraft are in every family somewhere in history if we dig back deep and far enough. There has been wickedness and sacrifice and worship of idols totally contrary to the Word of God. The only way to destroy it once and for all - over you and your children and seed even after is to MAKE

> No matter what kind of family you were brought up in or you currently have, that family does not define you. Nor does it dictate your future. The blood of Jesus cancels out the curse.

A CHOICE! That you will serve God and accept Him and His promises for you. The curse goes down to the 3rd and 4th generation but the blessing of God is to 1,000 generations! The curse is broken with you and you don't have to claim it for you or for your children! Be free daughter of dominion!

Exodus 20:5-6

> *"Thou shalt not bow down thyself to them, nor serve them: for I the Lord thy God am a jealous God, visiting the iniquity of the fathers upon the children unto the third and fourth generation of them that hate me; And shewing mercy unto thousands of them that love me, and keep my commandments."*

Deuteronomy 7:9

> *"Know therefore that the Lord thy God, he is God, the faithful God, which keepeth covenant and mercy with them that love him and keep his commandments to a thousand generations."*

The seed of a generation can be an impartation that works for a blessing and not a curse! In 1 Peter 3:6 *"Even as Sara obeyed Abraham, calling him lord: whose daughters ye are, as long as ye do well, and are not afraid with any amazement."*

You can choose whether you want to be a daughter of Delilah, a daughter of Michal, a daughter of Jezebel, a daughter of Vashti, a daughter of Potiphar's wife, or a daughter of Sarah. We covered earlier what a Proverbs 31 woman looks like. Here is a short list of women in the Bible you don't want to emulate. The traits they carry are the opposite of what a Daughter of Dominion walks in.

Delilah - (Judges Chapter 16) She was a Philistine who had bribed to entrap Samson, then coaxed him into revealing that the secret of his strength was his long hair, whereupon she took advantage of his confidence to betray him to his enemies. She has many wicked daughters. They are manipulating, deceptive, conniving. They'll see men completely taken out and cut off from the earth for self gain and reputation. Delilah is the woman that weakens men with poison, stripping them of their God-given strength and power for a moment of thrill and satisfaction.

Michal -This was a woman who was concerned more with false dignity and her appearance for and opinions of others than for honoring the Lord. We see her response to her husband, King David's extravagant worship in 2 Sam 6:14-16:

> *"and it was so, that when they that bare the ark of the Lord had gone six paces, he sacrificed oxen and fatlings.*
>
> *And David danced before the Lord with all his might; and David was girded with a linen ephod.*
>
> *So David and all the house of Israel brought up the ark of the Lord with shouting, and with the sound of the trumpet.*
>
> *And as the ark of the Lord came into the city of David, Michal Saul's daughter looked through a window, and saw king David leaping and dancing before the Lord; and she despised him in her heart."*

She literally hated her husband for worshipping the Lord because it didn't look "dignified" to her or others. She obviously cared more about how man looked at her than how God did. Her disrespect to God and her husband cost her dearly. Later in the chapter it reads: *Then David returned to bless his household. And Michal the daughter of Saul came out to meet David, and said, How glorious was the king of Israel to day, who uncovered himself* to day in the eyes of the handmaids of his servants, as one of the vain fellows shamelessly uncovereth himself!

> And David said unto Michal, It was before the Lord, which chose me before thy father, and before all his house, to appoint me ruler over the people of the Lord, over Israel: therefore will I play before the Lord. And I will yet be more vile than thus, and will be base in mine own sight: and of the maidservants which thou hast spoken of, of them shall I be had in honour. Therefore Michal the daughter of Saul had no child unto the day of her death. 2 Samuel 6:20-23

Unlike Michal, David cared not for his reputation before men. God's opinion is what mattered most. You will serve whom you fear. If you fear God you will serve him first. If you fear man then you will serve man. The Bible says: *the fear of man is a snare,But whoever trusts in the LORD shall be safe.*(Proverbs 29:25 NKJV) A snare is a trap and in this case it caused Michal to be barren the rest of her life.

Another trait we see in the seed of Michal is the utter disrespect for the anointing and the curse that it brings on women and men, even as we see this happening today. Mark those people that come against men of God and don't take part in their folly and disrespect. Shut them down. The Bible says in Psalms 105:15 *"Touch not mine anointed, and do my prophets no harm."* When people put their mouths on the prophets of God and come against the supernatural, their worship, hunger, giftings, or service unto the Lord, they are bringing a curse of barrenness into their own lives! Though they may produce children, those children will become fruit of their own seed. Every other aspect in their life you will see barrenness. Whatever they produce will be lifeless. I tell people all the time, that even if they may not agree with what a man or woman of God does, it's best to go to God about it and not criticize it, mock it, or gossip about it. There's a price to pay for dishonoring the anointing on a prophet of God's life! If you read the entire passage of Psalms 105, you see what happened to those who came against God's chosen children of Israel. It says in verse 16 that God struck the land with a famine because of what Joseph's brothers did to him. Their LAND was barren, cropless, dry, desolate, without life or fruit for 7 long years. It took them to come to repentance and to honor the man of God, in order to receive the fruit from the very life they harmed. Then what they sought to destroy became a blessing to them! Be careful what you criticize, mock, or hate. It could be the very thing that sets you free and gives you the breakthrough you've been praying for!

> Be careful what you criticize, mock, or hate. It could be the very thing that sets you free and gives you the breakthrough you've been praying for!

Jezebel - a woman from the Old Testament books of 1 & 2 Kings. She was the wife of King Ahab who ruled the kingdom of Israel. By opposing the worship of the Hebrew God Yahweh, neglecting the rights and well-being of her subjects, and challenging the great prophets Elijah and Elisha, she prompted the internal conflict that plagued Israel for decades. Her reign consisted of evil and tyrannical works. Jezebel has many daughters - Controlling, lying, using her beauty to persuade men to worship false idols.

The goal of Jezebel is to control the Government and to take out the Prophets of the Church of Jesus Christ. She wants to cut them off and deactivate the gift on their life, thereby seducing people into witchcraft and other means of the supernatural. Jezebel knows that if she can kill the Prophets, she can then destroy the Church. She is a deceiver and a manipulator that is best friends with Delilah. Jezebel is plagued with the spirit of lust and many men have fallen into her seductive traps, not knowing that the end is death. In the final end time church, I believe a lot of Jezebels and those carrying her wicked spirit are going to be cast out! God is coming back for a perfect and a spotless bride without blemish. Jezebel is being exposed by the Prophets and she is going out with the devil to his final destiny.

Vashti can be found in Esther Chapter 1-2:1. Vashti was very beautiful. Though she took a stand not to come to the King at his command to show off her beauty while he was drinking, her decision backfired and she was divinely dethroned and removed. She was used as an example of rebellion in all of the kingdom she once ruled in authority. She has many daughters, unfortunately. They are daughters of pride, false dignity, and selfishness. Unforgiveness causes Vashti to never heal due to the fact that everything revolves around her and she will not repent. There is in her an endless grudge which has hardened her heart. Her marriages are unstable and she sets a humiliating example for her husband. Vashti sets the tone for every woman under her to disrespect their husbands and to put self image and her own rights ahead of her husband's reputation. If Vashti doesn't repent, she will be replaced: in her marriage, her position of authority, and ultimately her respect that she has fought so hard and sacrificed everything just to keep. Vashti's behavior made way for Esther to deliver the Jews from death. It is obvious that Vashti's decision did not give her any victory. But it was used as an example against her of what ought not to be done. Vashti was not a wicked woman, she was just ignorant to the voice of the Holy Spirit.

Potiphar's wife is mentioned only in Genesis Chapter 39, the woman that worked relentlessly to seduce Joseph to lay with her, which he fled from her and she then framed and lied about him and he was sent to prison. She has many daughters. These are wicked women that are great seductresses. They are the adulterous women we read about in Proverbs 7, and the strange woman in Proverbs 5. She is sneaky, lustful, a liar, and unsatisfied with her husband. She cannot be trusted and is a poisonous viper in the Church. She craves for attention and affection. And cleverly pre-selects and stalks her prey. She is creatively scheming for ways to trap them. Her satisfaction is rooted in an addiction. The demon of lust in her is only temporarily satisfied with each sexual encounter that she has with another man in leadership (whether acted on or thought of). Whether single or married, this spirit of lust is craving for sexual attention and physical satisfaction. This is the mother and spirit behind women who proclaim to be saved and sanctified but wear their breasts and cleavages out in public and poke their lips out in photos, holding their bottoms out - all in hopes to seduce someone into temptation. These women need to be delivered from low self esteem and a spirit of lust. The Bible says that adultery begins in the heart - Matthew 5:27-28 *"Ye have heard that it was said by them of old time, Thou shalt not commit adultery: But I say unto you, That whosoever looketh on a woman to lust after her hath committed adultery with her already in his heart."* So you see, it's not about a physical commitment of adultery but it is a heart commitment of adultery. Potiphar's wife already committed adultery with Joseph in her heart. She craved him and the demons in her did not settle until she could have the opportunity to destroy him. Purity is always a matter of the heart. This is where it begins, and it will transfer into your actions, demeanor, speech and thoughts.

> Purity is always a matter of the heart. This is where it begins, and it will transfer into your actions, demeanor, speech and thoughts.

I remember a young lady saw me in Tampa Florida, right before I became an Associate Pastor and I was working on staff there at the Church after finishing Bible College. She said that she remembered meeting me in Baltimore and now something was different about me but she didn't know how to explain it. I then urged her to tell me. She said, "One word comes to mind. HOLINESS." That made me very happy. When other people can see that you have been delivered, you know it's real. Oh the power of deliverance at the Cross of Jesus Christ and time spent under the anointing, and in the fire of God! When you humble yourself and come broken, He can remake you to the woman of God that He intended for you to always be.

Sarah has many daughters! And I hope you desire to model and live as one of them! Let's look at the full passage in 1 Peter 3:

Likewise, ye wives, be in subjection to your own husbands; that, if any obey not the word, they also may without the word be won by the conversation of the wives;

While they behold your chaste conversation coupled with fear.

Whose adorning let it not be that outward adorning of plaiting the hair, and of wearing of gold, or of putting on of apparel;

> Sarah has many daughters! And I hope you desire to model and live as one of them!

But let it be the hidden man of the heart, in that which is not corruptible, even the ornament of a meek and quiet spirit, which is in the sight of God of great price.

For after this manner in the old time the holy women also, who trusted in God, adorned themselves, being in subjection unto their own husbands:

Even as Sara obeyed Abraham, calling him lord: whose daughters ye are, as long as ye do well, and are not afraid with any amazement."

When God called Abraham, the only direction he had was that God told him to "GO" and to take his wife to a place that He would show him. That's all He gave him. Can you just imagine the mouth that many women would give to their man today? She probably would ask him if he had lost his mind! Just paint the picture. Your husband comes to you and tells you that God is telling him to move and he has no further explanation or direction.

Then some time later, he tells you in your old age after you no longer have a menstrual cycle that you are going to have a baby. You try to stand in faith because it is your innermost secret desire of your heart. For 25 years it hasn't happened. And then, suddenly, when you are 99 years old your husband gets a visitation from angels that now is the time. And your womb is dead. All you can do is laugh! Through it all, Sarah still quietly trusted God and saw the promise come to fruition.

Sarah is a great woman of faith. She is an example of what a godly and submissive wife looks like, a beautiful portrait of a Daughter of King Jesus. We see within the above passage of 1 Peter 3:5-6 that Sarah adorned herself with a meek and quiet spirit, being in subjection to her own husband. And that without word she won him over. She called him lord and served him as royalty. She was to be the mother of many nations and he was to be the father of many nations. They go on record together as a couple, (the only couple mentioned in this passage) in Hebrews Chapter 11, in the Great Biblical Hall of Faith. May you and your husband go on record as a couple that makes history!

We see in Hebrews 11:11 *"Through faith also Sara herself received strength to conceive seed, and was delivered of a child when she was past age, because she judged him faithful who had promised."* She very well could have died in child bearing. Not only was her womb dead, but her body was weak and her organs were declining. She did not have the strength of a young woman. But the Bible says she was STRONG IN FAITH. She had a supernatural strength, her strength coming from a greater realm. She knew that her Faithful God, who promised her a son, was bringing His promise to pass! A woman's strength comes from her obedience to God's Word and her submission to her husband. Submission is not weakness, it is strength. A strong woman does not need to stand up to her man but she stands beside him and is the helpmate God created her to be, to help him to fulfill his God-given task.

> May you and your husband go on record as a couple that makes history!

The word submission used to scare me. Being an 'independent woman' for so many years, I did not want to surrender all my rights, or to be controlled by anyone or in subjection to their decisions. Especially after many men had already failed me. I got so nervous thinking of how I would be told what I couldn't wear anymore or who I couldn't hang out with or how to spend my money. I realized that this feeling was rooted in fear. When I got married to a man of God I had to let those thoughts go and take them captive and learn how to trust my husband. As I did, I realized that God actually used him to help deliver me from things I didn't even realize I needed to be delivered from. There's power in obedience to God's Word. God favors his daughters when we trust Him. When we trust God, we can trust our husbands. Because we know the God in them is the same God that has adopted us as His daughters and loves us unconditionally, as He loves them. I believe that as you take Sarah as the model of holiness, reverence and respect for her husband, and faith in God, and make the necessary changes, your marriage will go to the next level, the desires of your heart will come to pass, and God will give you a testimony that is nothing short of supernatural.

> God actually used him to help deliver me from things I didn't even realize I needed to be delivered from.

Let's close this Chapter with looking at Galatians 3:6-14:

Even as Abraham believed God, and it was accounted to him for righteousness.

Know ye therefore that they which are of faith, the same are the children of Abraham.

And the scripture, foreseeing that God would justify the heathen through faith, preached before the gospel unto Abraham, saying, In thee shall all nations be blessed.

So then they which be of faith are blessed with faithful Abraham.

For as many as are of the works of the law are under the curse: for it is written, Cursed is every one that continueth not in all things which are written in the book of the law to do them.

But that no man is justified by the law in the sight of God, it is evident: for, The just shall live by faith.

And the law is not of faith: but, The man that doeth them shall live in them.

Christ hath redeemed us from the curse of the law, being made a curse for us: for it is written, Cursed is every one that hangeth on a tree:

That the blessing of Abraham might come on the Gentiles through Jesus Christ; that we might receive the promise of the Spirit through faith.

So we can see according to the Word of God that we are children of Abraham when we have faith in Jesus Christ and become saved. WE are the nations that are blessed through Abraham's covenant. Jesus went to the Cross so that we can be freed from the curse of the Law. The Law brought a curse. There it stopped short. That was all it could do. Jesus Christ undid the result of the Law by delivering us from the curse.

Because the Lord redeemed us, the blessing of Abraham can be ours. And we can receive the promise of the Spirit through faith. Make the right choice for yourself and for your generation today!!

Workbook Section, Chapter 4:

1. Why is it that the devil was after the seed of the woman from the beginning?

   _____

   _____

   _____

   _____

2. The power of the seed is in its _____. We can find this to be true as it is explained in John 12:24.

3. What generational curses have been broken over your family because of the fact that you are under the blessing as a child of God?

   _____

   _____

   _____

   _____

Now, speak and declare this: *"The curse of _____ is broken over me and my family in the name of Jesus! The curse of _____ is broken over me and my family in the name of Jesus! The blood of Jesus has cancelled out the curse! And the blessing is greater to 1,000 generations of my seed! I bless my body, I bless my life, I bless my children, I bless my husband and I bless all of my grandchildren and all of their lives! Nothing can take the blessing away from us. I bind every plan of the wicked one and command it to backfire in Jesus' name! I activate the blessing and speak divine increase into every realm of our lives in the mighty name of Jesus! Long life, great health, wholeness, sound minds, righteousness and prosperity is our portion! The Blessing is Greater!!! Hallelujah"*

4. As a "daughter of Sarah", what are some of the key things that stick out to you about her character that you would like to have in your life?

_____

_____

_____

_____

_____

_____

_____

Chapter 5

The Gift of a Woman: to Her Husband, to Her Children, & to Her World

Let's look at Proverbs 31. The woman in this Chapter was a portrait of what King Solomon's mother gave to him in what type of woman he should be selecting as his wife. This is the model of a potential Queen, a King's wife. We can see in this passage, examples of the gift this woman was to her husband, her children, and also to her world.

Proverbs 31:10-31

Who can find a virtuous woman? for her price is far above rubies.

The heart of her husband doth safely trust in her, so that he shall have no need of spoil.

She will do him good and not evil all the days of her life.

She seeketh wool, and flax, and worketh willingly with her hands.

She is like the merchants' ships; she bringeth her food from afar.

She riseth also while it is yet night, and giveth meat to her household, and a portion to her maidens.

She considereth a field, and buyeth it: with the fruit of her hands she planteth a vineyard.

She girdeth her loins with strength, and strengtheneth her arms.

She perceiveth that her merchandise is good: her candle goeth not out by night.

She layeth her hands to the spindle, and her hands hold the distaff.

She stretcheth out her hand to the poor; yea, she reacheth forth her hands to the needy.

She is not afraid of the snow for her household: for all her household are clothed with scarlet.

She maketh herself coverings of tapestry; her clothing is silk and purple.

Her husband is known in the gates, when he sitteth among the elders of the land.

She maketh fine linen, and selleth it; and delivereth girdles unto the merchant.

Strength and honour are her clothing; and she shall rejoice in time to come.

She openeth her mouth with wisdom; and in her tongue is the law of kindness.

She looketh well to the ways of her household, and eateth not the bread of idleness.

Her children arise up, and call her blessed; her husband also, and he praiseth her.

Many daughters have done virtuously, but thou excellest them all.

Favour is deceitful, and beauty is vain: but a woman that feareth the Lord, she shall be praised.

Give her of the fruit of her hands; and let her own works praise her in the gates.

To Her Husband:

Looking back in the very beginning, God sets out His divine purpose for the woman - created to be a helpmate to her husband. Genesis 2:18, *"And the Lord God said, It is not good that the man should be alone; I will make him a help meet for him."* God said He would make another human being suitable to meet man's needs and to assist him in his calling, and all aspects of life. The wife compliments, corresponds, and helps her husband. In Proverbs 18:22 it says, *"Whoso findeth a wife findeth a good thing, and obtaineth favour of the Lord"*. We can also see from this scripture that a woman is a gift to man, bringing FAVOR from the Lord because she is there by his side. A wife is a good thing! She is not a trap, she is a precious gift! Even if right now you feel inadequate to be a wife, know right now and settle right now that you are a gift to your husband. As women we have to ensure that we are fulfilling our God-given role as our husband's helpmate and not as his mother or boss and most definitely not a hindrance to him and his calling. We should be lovingly helping and encouraging them forward into their purpose and not holding them backwards with our own doubt and fear. A woman carries a powerful influence and because God created us to help our husbands, many men have been led astray by women not walking in and yielding to the Holy Spirit. Look at what happened in Genesis Chapter 3. Eve persuaded her husband to eat the forbidden fruit that God had already commanded him not to eat of. Once they both ate of the fruit, they were kicked out of the Garden naked, and died a spiritual death (separated from the

> A wife is a good thing! She is not a trap, she is a precious gift!

presence of God). Their sin not only affected their children but for generations and generations to come. We can see the influence of Delilah to Samson in the book of Judges and how she persuaded him into sharing the secret of his strength and it ultimately killed him. A wrong wife can be detrimental to her husband. But I believe I am speaking to women that will be a blessing to their husbands and who will rise up to be an even greater gift to them in the days to come!

When my husband and I were courting, we were just beginning Bible College. There were many times where he wanted to quit. I could have supported those feelings he was having of insecurity and doubt in the call on his life. Instead, I saw a big picture. I saw what he could be in Christ and how God could use him in His kingdom. I encouraged him every day and shared with him the things that I saw. He will tell you today how much this helped him to stick in the race. Only Jesus gets the credit for anything good that has come out of our lives. But the fact is, God used me as a woman (his wife to be) to help him to fulfill his divine purpose.

It is your job as his wife to ensure you are helping and not hindering. Remember Proverbs 14:1, *"Every wise woman buildeth her house: but the foolish plucketh it down with her hands."* And Proverbs 18:21 says *"Death and life are in the power of the tongue: and they that love it shall eat the fruit therof."* Use your tongue to build your husband and not to tear him down. Your words can be used to sustain him or to kill him. To increase him or to decrease him. To encourage or to discourage. Perhaps he is not doing what you feel he ought to be doing, or involved in what you want him involved in right now. Ask God to open your spiritual eyes to His call. You can by the Spirit of God encourage him in that area of what you see for his life. Also know that God is speaking to him also. Your support is key as well as him knowing

> Use your tongue to build your husband and not to tear him down.

that you are with him and believe in him and will do whatever you need to do to help him. Remember, you are there to help him, not to control him.

God-ordained order in the home is very critical. God is first, then man, then woman, then children. Children do not control their parents, and a woman does not run her man. The husband is the head of the home, and his wife is his helpmate and the keeper of her home. As long as God is first, the entire home functions properly and disorder is not going to be your portion.

In Proverbs 31, let's hit some key verses concerning the gift that a wife is to her husband. We will be discussing it in AMPC (Amplified Classic Edition)

Verse 11

The heart of her husband trusts in her confidently and relies on and believes in her securely, so that he has no lack of [honest] gain or need of [dishonest] spoil.

Because her husband can fully trust her, he can rely on her and have total and complete confidence in her. Therefore, he knows that the finances are in order and there is no lack in his home. The finances that come in are honest and true. He trusts that she is not out doing dishonest transactions and hurting his name and keeping a good report for the family.

Verse 12

She comforts, encourages, and does him only good as long as there is life within her.

Notice the power of a woman's tongue in this one verse. With our mouth we can comfort, encourage and do good to our husband. All of her life, as long as she is alive, meaning all of her days. You won't find her gossiping and complaining about her husband. She is not hurting him with her tongue. I know of an amazing woman of God and widow that to this day, she only speaks good of her husband. She praises him for the husband

and father he was, even as he is gone into eternity. You have some women, when their husband dies, using their death as an opportunity to come out with the truth of how "lazy", "sloppy", and "good for nothing" they were. Ladies, there is no perfect man. We all have fallen short. You may be picking up those socks daily, or cleaning the toilet or sink from him one time too many, or getting tired of making all of his meals, and sometimes even feeling weary with pleasing him physically. But you know what, these things come with being a WIFE. They are a privilege and an honor. We cannot be selfish. There will come a day when one of you will die first. And you don't want to have any regrets. Cherish everyday that you get to serve your husband. And do it with excellence. Remember, there are women out there who their heart's cry is that God will bless them with a husband. Don't become a Vashti and be arrogant and get replaced by someone humble enough to serve him and be the wife he deserves.

Verse 15

"She rises while it is yet night and gets [spiritual] food for her household and assigns her maids their tasks."

This gift of a woman is willing to lose a little bit of sleep to hear from heaven concerning her husband and her children. She seeks God in the Secret Place and gets her time in under the anointing. She is a praying woman and she has her war room space! Ladies, in order to pour out, you have to get poured into. You cannot feed others or nourish others from a dry well. She even pours spiritually into her maidens and plans their work for the day. She is full of heaven's divine orders for her day and for her family. She can strengthen her husband spiritually and not weaken him spiritually because she knows how to pray and she lives in the Spirit.

Verse 16-18

She considers a [new] field before she buys or accepts it [expanding prudently and not courting neglect of her present duties by assuming other duties]; with her savings [of time and strength] she plants fruitful vines in her vineyard.

She girds herself with strength [spiritual, mental, and physical fitness for her God-given task] and makes her arms strong and firm.

She tastes and sees that her gain from work [with and for God] is good; her lamp goes not out, but it burns on continually through the night [of trouble, privation, or sorrow, warning away fear, doubt, and distrust].

The gift of a woman does not neglect her household or her husband by taking on other duties that leave them without. She keeps herself strong spiritually, mentally and physically for her God-given task as a helpmate and a mother.

Her lamp does not go out! It burns continuously! She maintains her fire, passion and zeal! She is full of the fire of God and no matter the night or the challenges that come her way or tries to come near her husband or family, she does not lose her fire or her faith or strength. Her light shines for her household and for her world. She is consistent. Not spiritually strong and joyful today, then weak and depressed tomorrow. This woman can be counted on, always willing and ready to pour out and to strengthen others spiritually.

Matthew 5:16 says, *"Let your light so shine before men, that they may see your good works, and glorify your Father which is in heaven."*

Verses 21-23

She fears not the snow for her family, for all her household are doubly clothed in scarlet.

She makes for herself coverlets, cushions, and rugs of tapestry. Her clothing is of linen, pure and fine, and of purple [such as that of which the clothing of the priests and the hallowed cloths of the temple were made].

Her husband is known in the [city's] gates, when he sits among the elders of the land.

This woman takes care of the needs of her entire family. Neither her, nor her children are dressed in rags. They are dressed in clean and neat material, fine and top of the line. She is modest and virtuous but she also doesn't walk around looking homely and like a rag doll. She is attractive to her HUSBAND. She adorns herself to please him and her God.

Her husband has a great reputation and is well known in the city. He is a man of high leadership and authority. She compliments him and doesn't take away from him. A lot of people use the term "she married up" or "he married up". But this is not even biblical. So, are they saying the other person "married down"? A wife is a HELP MATE in every way. A man is a LEADER, to be cultivating and dressing and adding to his wife, covering and strengthening her spiritually as well. He is the Bishop and Overseer of their home. We aren't to be unequally yoked with an unbeliever (See 2 Corinthians 6:14). The only way anyone has married down is if they married an unbeliever or an individual who was not walking with Jesus. If however this is the case, it is their believing spouse's job to do everything they can to win them into the kingdom of God and to bring them up to their God-given position in the home and in the world.

Looking at 1 Peter 3:1, it says, *"Likewise, ye wives, be in subjection to your own husbands; that, if any obey not the word, they also may* without the word *be won by the conversation of the wives."*

The Amplified version says, *".......they may be won over not by discussion but by the [godly] lives of their wives."*

Sometimes we think that we have to fix the problem by justifying things with him with words or by "nagging" him about it or just being constant day by day putting it before our husbands. But the Bible says the total opposite to be true. I once heard a story of a woman whose husband was unsaved but she was saved and loved Jesus. She wanted with everything in her for him to be changed and to follow Jesus. So, she would preach the Gospel to him regularly and anything else she could do to be a witness. Nothing was working. She got no results. Finally, she went to God and He showed her the above passage. She decided to stop doing what she was doing and just to love him and serve him. Within months, he came to be saved and was following after Jesus right along with her. She got a revelation on this passage! Preaching to your husband won't change him. But loving him and serving him will bring him into the kingdom. As you focus on Jesus and His Word, and just pray for your husband and love and honor and respect him, you will reap the rewards of your obedience!

To Her Children:

As we begin to look at a woman's role to her children, let's start from the very beginning. A woman's child is her child the moment she conceives. It's supernatural how a woman can sense that she is with a child even before she misses her menstrual or takes a pregnancy test. She loves and is connected spiritually to the baby from the very start. I have loved all of my children from the moment I even thought they were in my womb. During the pregnancy of my firstborn, I felt connected to her more than I have ever felt connected to anyone in my life before. I was in awe that there was literally another human being living on the inside of me. However, I could feel the entire pregnancy that something was wrong. After my bloodwork and sonogram, I received a call from the doctor that she had a high chance of having Trisomy 21(commonly known as Down Syndrome).

They then proceeded to tell me my option to have an amnio-centesis (a test of the amniotic fluid to determine abnormalities). They said if she tested positive for it, I could have an abortion. There was no way that I was going to abort my baby! My first fruit and the beat of my heart, the little person growing and fluttering on the inside of me. I could feel her already moving and my belly was growing bigger by the week. Even though I was curious to have the testing done, I did not want to risk the needle aborting the baby that would go into my stomach to test her. There were many reports I had read about where this happened. I went through the entire rest of the pregnancy, feeling that something wasn't right. When she was born, she ended up testing positive for the chromosome abnormality and diagnosis. Physically the labor had drained me, going through a long natural labor and ending up having to be rushed in for an emergency c-section.

When she was just 2 weeks old, I was going through post-partum depression. My legs and feet were still swollen from the epidural and my stomach was still in excruciating pain. I was getting no sleep at night, and I felt helpless. My precious mother in law flew in when she was born and stayed with us several weeks, feeding her and helping all she could around the house. Our church family came over daily, showering us in love and support, bringing meals and diapers to the house. This is when all the nightmares began. I would have dream upon dream of children with all kinds of disabilities, of all races and genders. One, in particular, I remember is one where the devil was in a rocking chair laughing and holding a baby that was bleeding. I never forgot it. I knew that the devil thought he had won the battle over my baby and that his plan was to destroy her. (John 10:10).

Things begin to change from that moment. I got angry, mad, drew a line in the sand and there was a major shift in my faith! I realized just how beautiful my baby was and how tender and precious she was and began enjoying every moment with her. My body was also starting to recover. I found that I stopped smiling through the pain, but I actually had real joy. I was actually ready to go out of the house and face real life again. I was going to show and prove the devil wrong and to be the liar that he was. He would not win and there was no way I was going to give up and allow a doctor's report to dictate the future of my child. Everything they said she could never do, she was going to do. Every health problem they told me she would have, she would NEVER have. She would live a long and healthy life. To this day, my firstborn at 8 years old has zero health problems, is reading, writing, and doing everything that man said she could not do. She met every developmental milestone and is flourishing spiritually and in all aspects of life. The half has yet been told!

I do not accept anything but the report of the Lord. I don't identify her as what the world identifies her as. She is the healed of the Lord and that is all that we confess. Whatever you confess over your children is what you are going to receive. She is truly a living miracle!

When I found out I was pregnant with my second child, I didn't have a pregnancy test or any other signs. I just knew it. I remember looking to the sky and crying and asking God how I was going to do this. My firstborn was 5.5 months at the time and we were in the middle of our Internship in Bible College, and facing a very difficult time financially and I was somewhat still struggling with the natural facts of the diagnosis from my firstborn. I had wondered how I could really parent another child when the doctors said she would need so much attention. And how they said that all of our children or 50% of them could have the same diagnosis. I was afraid, concerned, worried, and emotional. I went into the bathroom alone to cry again and I remember the love of God flooding that room and He assured me that He would take care of us and that this baby was a gift that He was giving to me. I knew that a gift you can take or you can refuse. And I chose to take the gift.

The love and the joy of the Lord filled me to overflowing and I came out completely free. Immediately, we went and got a pregnancy test and we were so happy about the good news and told everyone we could! The devil worked hard to taunt me the entire pregnancy with fear and nightmares and thoughts of the worst things that could happen with her health. I rebuked them again and again! Finally, I talked to a Pastor, a great woman of God, that gave me great advice to seek God alone for a Word for this child's health. I decided to go into my prayer closet. Right away, as I opened my Bible it landed on Psalm 91 and my eyes went straight to verse 10. I forgot about ever seeing that verse before, "There shall NO EVIL befall thee, neither shall any plague come nigh thy dwelling." God's Word is personal for YOU. And when you seek answers in His Word, He will give them to you. I stood on that Word throughout the entire pregnancy. Just the fact that the devil doesn't want you to do something or is bombarding you in fear, shows you that he sees the victory on the other side. His goal is to discourage you out of the victory. He wants to destroy your testimony! Don't let him! Stand in faith for your children regardless!

I increased in faith and in joy and in confidence. The nightmares ceased and my second born baby was born completely healthy and whole and beautiful as ever! And every single thing she needed when she was born came in supernaturally and she and none of our house has lacked a single day.

I had a tragic miscarriage my 3rd pregnancy. Not only did I receive a positive pregnancy test, but I knew, that I knew ,that I knew in my spirit that I was pregnant. I remember bleeding profusely and in a single large amount. I ended up going to the hospital and they discharged me with a miscarriage. When it happened I cried and couldn't believe something like that could happen to us. God spoke to me that He had a very special baby that I was to have and that the baby we lost was in heaven. It was tough to think about and I felt like a part of me was missing. I began to love my other 2 children even more.

Without even realizing it, I then became pregnant with my 3rd child and my 4th pregnancy. By the time I realized I was pregnant with her she was 8 weeks. I had not one nightmare with her and not one concern. When I got my bloodwork done, they told me she was average to high risk of having the same diagnosis as our firstborn. The devil was too late! Our faith was so strong at this point, that I never second guessed the word of the Lord. When the thoughts would even try to come I would rebuke them and stand on the Word in Psalm 91:10 that held me before. She was born beautiful and completely whole.

God gave man and woman a commision to be fruitful and to multiply and replenish the earth and subdue it. We cannot be paralyzed with fear. After I was recovered and strengthened in faith from my firstborn and received the Word of the Lord for my second born, I made up my mind on that, I was NOT going to allow the devil to stop me from having babies and I would make him out to be the liar he was! We would have as many babies as we wanted to and everytime God would get the glory! *Children are a blessing from the Lord! And the fruit of the womb is HIS reward!* Psalm 127:3

The Power of the Womb:

As a woman we have been given a womb. (Yes, we already know this but let's actually think about that). This is very significant to her role as a woman and the blessing she can be to her children and to those assigned to her life to nurture. A woman is one of a kind and truly this comes from her physical makeup and functions, given to her thoughtfully and uniquely by the Creator.

Look at this beautiful passage:

Psalm 139:13-18

For thou hast possessed my reins: thou hast covered me in my mother's womb.

I will praise thee; for I am fearfully and wonderfully made: marvellous are thy works; and that my soul knoweth right well.

My substance was not hid from thee, when I was made in secret, and curiously wrought in the lowest parts of the earth.

Thine eyes did see my substance, yet being unperfect; and in thy book all my members were written, which in continuance were fashioned, when as yet there was none of them.

How precious also are thy thoughts unto me, O God! how great is the sum of them!

If I should count them, they are more in number than the sand: when I awake, I am still with thee.

Your baby is supernaturally protected and knit together by God Himself in your womb. Every part was created in secret, fearfully and wonderfully.

The function of the womb, according to the Encyclopaedia Britannica, is "to nourish and house a fertilized egg until the fetus, or offspring, is ready to be delivered." Every single human being that has ever been alive on the planet - both now and in all of time, has achieved its existence through this organ. Even Jesus Himself had to be born through the natural means of a woman. Though He was conceived of the Spirit and came from heaven, the womb of Mary was held strong by God Himself, where every detail was formed.

There have been babies born supernaturally to women without a womb and this is a miracle even greater. In many cases, God even created a womb just to keep the baby inside of its mother. No matter the case, it is GOD Almighty that has kept them. Maybe you need a miracle in your womb or the doctor has declared you "barren". Barrenness is not a part of the covenant that God has established for you. God said in Deuteronomy 28:4, 11. "***Blessed shall be the fruit of thy body***, *and the fruit of thy ground, and the fruit of thy cattle, the increase of thy kine, and the flocks of thy sheep." "And the LORD shall make thee plenteous in goods,* in the fruit of thy body, *and in the fruit of thy cattle, and in the fruit of thy ground, in the land which the Lord sware unto thy fathers to give thee."*

Barrenness was nailed to the cross! I have prayed with 3 women before that had no menstrual cycle: one of them hadn't had one her entire life and she was in her 20s, one hadn't had one since she was a teenager, and the other hadn't in over 3 years. I could tangibly feel the anointing coming out of my hands and into their stomachs. Within days, every single one of them contacted me to tell me that their menstrual cycle started! We even prayed for a woman at an outreach crusade that the doctors had told her the baby in her womb was dead. After prayer, she felt the baby moving and kicking again! There have been countless times that women who could not conceive a baby received prayer and supernaturally within months became pregnant! I remember trying for 8 months before we got pregnant with our first. It wasn't long looking back, compared to how long so many others have waited. But at the time it seemed forever. I even started taking natural fertility herbs. It wasn't until I forgot to be taking them that I got pregnant!

God has declared in His Word that you are fruitful and will be made a joyful mother of children!

Psalm 113:9 *"He maketh the barren woman to keep house, and to be a joyful mother of children."*

Submission to Authority begins in the womb! You have the power in you to speak life over your baby and what they will be in Christ. They will submit to your authority as their mother, before they even learn to speak. Your words carry power and the backing of all of heaven. Speak the Word and pray over them even as they are growing inside of you. They hear every word! Babies learn the anointing and recognize it, even from the womb! Look at Luke 1:41 - *"And it came to pass, that, when Elizabeth heard the salutation of Mary, the baby leaped in her womb; and Elizabeth was filled with the Holy Ghost."* When Elizabeth came into contact with the anointing, her baby John the Baptist leaped inside her and kicked. And she began to prophesy! Don't underestimate the anointing in a child. They will respond to the anointing.

It is God's will for you to have children. Stand fast onto His Word and don't let it go. I break every plague of barrenness off of the daughters of God and command every womb and womanly organ to function at its full capacity and for every desire of every couple that is believing God for children to come to pass in Jesus' name!!!

A womb gives birth to that which lives and even to those things which may be dead. Either way, it must come through the womb.

What does this tell us? That a woman has power within her to birth things into existence! Things that may be dead or inactive, hidden in secret. But she can bring them out to the open and into the world for its intended purpose. Look at Mary the mother of Jesus. She pushed Jesus into His very first miracle.

John 2:1-11

> *And the third day there was a marriage in Cana of Galilee; and the mother of Jesus was there:*
>
> *And both Jesus was called, and his disciples, to the marriage.*
>
> *And when they wanted wine, the mother of Jesus saith unto him, They have no wine.*
>
> *Jesus saith unto her, Woman, what have I to do with thee? mine hour is not yet come.*
>
> *His mother saith unto the servants, Whatsoever he saith unto you, do it.*
>
> *And there were set there six waterpots of stone, after the manner of the purifying of the Jews, containing two or three firkins apiece.*
>
> *Jesus saith unto them, Fill the waterpots with water. And they filled them up to the brim.*
>
> *And he saith unto them, Draw out now, and bear unto the governor of the feast. And they bare it.*
>
> *When the ruler of the feast had tasted the water that was made wine, and knew not whence it was: (but the servants which drew the water knew;) the governor of the feast called the bridegroom,*
>
> *And saith unto him, Every man at the beginning doth set forth good wine; and when men have well drunk, then that which is worse: but thou hast kept the good wine until now.*

This beginning of miracles did Jesus in Cana of Galilee, and manifested forth his glory; and his disciples believed on him.

At conception: the man plants. And the woman nurtures, feeds and nourishes that seed to grow.

The Bible says *"I have planted, Apollos watered; but God gave the increase."* 1 Corinthians 3:6

God uses both men and women to multiply and bring forth seed into the earth. Each is truly intricate to their seed and the effect of that seed in the world. Not everybody can plant and not everybody can water just one individual and ALL increase comes from God. It is He alone that works in a woman to bless her womb and her God-given ability to water and to nourish and sustain. Everything good that comes from a woman is always attributed to Her Creator.

A woman is a gift to her children because she has everything within her, perfectly put together by an All Powerful All Knowing God needed to raise them up in the Lord to fulfill heaven's purpose.

As a parent, your children have been stewarded to you. You only have them temporarily. And it is your full responsibility and honor to raise them up in the fear and admonition of the Lord (Ephesians 6:4). We are stewarded with their very lives - with their eternal destiny. It is our responsibility, as parents, to guarantee our children make it into heaven.

The Bible says if we train them in the way they should go, when they are old, they will not depart from it (Proverbs 22:6). This verse does not mean that every child is guaranteed to backslide. I remember sitting at a Minister's Luncheon with some ladies and one of them was talking about how her son backslid but is now serving Jesus. She then said "Well you know they all will go their own way and usually they do backslide, but they'll eventually come back around." I said boldly, "My children will never backslide." I wasn't trying to be arrogant, or rude. I told her that I believe we would get exactly what we spoke and had faith for. She eventually agreed.

We have already declared that our children will serve the Lord all their days of their lives and never backslide. As a matter of fact, we have prayed it over them every night of their lives. They hear us declare it over them and they have it embedded into their spirits. They will tell you that they will always serve Jesus. We refuse to confess that our children will make our same mistakes. They will not know drugs and alcohol, prison, fornication, or adultery. Even if you are a mom who got saved after you came to the Lord, you can declare this over your children that recently became saved. If they aren't serving Jesus now, hold fast to His Word! He hastens His Word to perform it! The Bible says in 2 Peter 3:9 *"The Lord is not slack concerning His promise, as some count slackness, but is longsuffering toward us, not willing that any should perish but that all should come to repentance"*. If we have failed in raising them to serve the Lord, we can pick back up. Maybe your children are adults and they are not serving Jesus for any given reason. Through your own life and example and your unfailing prayers and love, you can win them into the kingdom. Your love to them, and to your husband, if you are married, will draw them to Jesus. God loves prodigals (those kids that have left home spiritually and are wasting their lives: time and money, not serving the Lord). The Bible says he is married to the backslider (Jeremiah 3:14). Even when I was out partying as a prodigal daughter, God was always there. I could feel He was there and I was always convicted because my parents had already instilled the Word in me. Be encouraged, that as you continue to pray in faith, your prayers will be answered and they are guaranteed to come back to Jesus and begin to live for Him. Remember, He wants them saved even more than you want them saved and serving Jesus!

There are many ways that we can raise our children in the fear and admonition of the Lord, that can guarantee them success in life. Let's go to the Word of God:

Proverbs 29:15

> *"The rod and reproof give wisdom: but a child left to himself bringeth his mother to shame."*

Proverbs 23:13-14

> *"Withhold not correction from the child: for if thou beatest him with the rod, he shall not die. Thou shalt beat him with the rod, and shalt deliver his soul from hell."*

Proverbs 13:24

> *"He that spareth his rod hateth his son: but he that loveth him chasteneth him betimes."*

We can see here that it is imperative that you discipline your children. When you decide not to discipline them, they bring you shame. When you discipline your children, the Bible says you deliver their soul from hell. This is the key to their eternal success.

From the time a child is two you can use even a little wooden spoon. And increase it in size as they are older. Obviously, by the time a child is 13, you shouldn't have to keep spanking their bottoms. If you are diligent and consistent in your discipline and teaching and raising them, by the time they are teenagers they will be able to discern their actions and between good and evil and know the voice of the Holy Spirit. Keeping a good relationship with your children is so key. You never want to physically abuse them. Any spankings should be done in a closed room away from other people and with the intent of spanking. It should never be out of anger or lashing out or smacking children across the heads.

My Pastor's mother, Granny, in Tampa gave great advice that I still practice to this day. She said that we should take the child aside, explain to them what they did wrong and what the Bible says about their actions and how it is sin and it put Jesus on the cross. Next give them a scripture from the Bible on discipline. Then tell them you are going to spank them. Next, have them repent. After they've repented, tell them that you also forgive them and that you love them. Lastly, hug and kiss them and ensure their attitude is adjusted and they leave at peace and with joy, knowing that God is pleased with them. This is critical when they are little because you are setting the foundation for their spankings. I promise it seemed like I was spanking all of them 10 times a day for the same things. But now, things have gotten a lot easier.

We only spank for specific things and that is lying, disobedience, or intentionally hurting one another physically. When kids break things or cry or argue with one another over a toy, they are just being kids. That's when you come in to redirect their energy and mediate the situation in love.

As important as it is to discipline children, I want to emphasize that it is imperative that you love on them 20 times more. Ensure that you are not always talking negatively to your children, complaining to them and nagging them and saying everything they aren't. Speak life to them and over them and speak in the contrary to what they are doing. For instance, if your child is not attentive during family worship time, or if they are having trouble with their grades, always speak life in that area to them. Encourage them by saying things like, "You are going to be an amazing worshipper. I see it in you!" Or, "God is giving you such a great hunger for His presence, honey." For their schoolwork, say "You will ace this thing! You are smart and this is going to be so easy compared to all God is going to use you for!" "You can be whatever you want in life!" "You are Mommy's Superstar!" "We are so proud of you." "You are a blessing." "I am so glad God gave me you."

Learn how your child best receives love and cover them in love. A child needs natural affection, undivided attention and quality time with their parents.

Also, children don't always do exactly what you say they should do. Children will do exactly what you do. You can't tell them to live and act one way and you are acting totally opposite. You may have heard the saying "the apple doesn't fall far from the tree." Don't be a person that would grieve you to see in your children.

Another thing I want to emphasize about parenting, is that you should never compare your children to one another. As you train them to hear the voice of the Holy Spirit, they will learn how to follow that voice in their own lives. It is our job to guide, raise and direct them in the ways of the Lord so that when they are old they will not depart and they can know what their purpose is in life. We cannot choose their career or profession. We cannot even choose for them whether they will go into the ministry. Going into the ministry is not a choice, it is a calling. We want them to obey God and to do what He has set out for them to do. That is where their success and blessing lies.

You children are not a burden. They are a blessing! They don't slow you down or cause you to miss out! Nor did they come in and ruin your life. I would not be the person I am today if it wasn't for my children. Nor, would I even know this inkling of the love that the Father has for me, if I didn't have my own. Your children are not a mistake. Your boys were not supposed to be your girls and your girls were not supposed to be any boys. They are exactly what God predestined them to be! For His purpose and glory. Your prayer should be that they exceed everything good that both you and their father ever did and ever will. Your success as a parent lies in their future success, as your seed. They are precious gifts to you and you are a gift to them. You both are gifts to God to glorify Him and to share His love with the world. Believe that God gave you everything you need to be their Mom. Because He did! And you can do this! You were born for it!

Look at Psalm 127:3-5

> *Lo, children are an heritage of the LORD; and the fruit of the womb is his reward.*
>
> *As arrows are in the hand of a mighty man; so are children of the youth.*
>
> *Happy is the man that hath his quiver full of them: they shall not be ashamed, but they shall speak with the enemies in the gate.*

For hundreds and thousands of years, women have been rais-ing children at home that have become great and historic icons and heroes. Women have raised Doctors, Presidents, Inventors, Teachers, Scientists, Evangelists, Missionaries, Pastors, Apostles, and Prophets. This shows us that we have everything needed in us to see our world changed. Look at this lovely example here:

Evangelist John Wesley who led a Revival movement in the Church of England in the 1700s, which sparked the Methodist movement, had a mom that helped set the course of his future. His mom, Susanna, had 19 children, of which 9 survived past infancy. What a strong woman to have lost 10 babies and still have the strength to run her household and to raise a Revivalist! She raised all of her children at home. Each child was taught to read as soon as they could walk and talk. They were expected to become proficient in Latin and Greek and to have learned major portions of the New Testament by heart. Susanna Wesley examined each child before the midday meal and before evening prayers. The children were not allowed to eat between meals and were interviewed singly by their mother one evening each week for the purpose of intensive spiritual instruction. Wow! Talk about order and being a keeper of her home. She also had a time slot of 1-2pm each day, where she would go into her room and lock her door. She was getting into her Secret Place with God and having her personal devotion. Every child knew not to come near that door, or it would not be well with them.

Personal devotion is key to being able to feed our children spiritually and to be the wife and woman that God has destined us to be.

The Gift of a Woman to her World:

The woman has a powerful position on this earth. She is equally called to multiply, bear fruit, dominate and subdue the EARTH. She is called to a high and holy calling! To be a light, to be a witness, and an ambassador of the King! A woman is a gift to her family, her generation and to her entire world. By her influence into just one child or just one man, or one young girl

- the effects can be unending. She is also a gift to her local church body, as she brings talents and skills that can build and strengthen the body of Christ and reach others with the love of Jesus. For this section, I really want to key in on Matthew 25:35-39. This is Jesus speaking:

For I was an hungred, and ye gave me meat: I was thirsty, and ye gave me drink: I was a stranger, and ye took me in:

Naked, and ye clothed me: I was sick, and ye visited me: I was in prison, and ye came unto me.

Then shall the righteous answer him, saying, Lord, when saw we thee an hungred, and fed thee? or thirsty, and gave thee drink?

When saw we thee a stranger, and took thee in? or naked, and clothed thee?

Or when saw we thee sick, or in prison, and came unto thee?

And the King shall answer and say unto them, Verily I say unto you, Inasmuch as ye have done it unto one of the least of these my brethren, ye have done it unto me.

God promised Abraham that He would bless him and would also MAKE HIM A BLESSING (Genesis 12:2)! God not only wants to bless you and your household. He wants to make you a dispenser of goods to others!

A woman is a BLESSING! She is not a sexual object to this world but a blessing to this world. She is more than someone barefoot and pregnant, someone to serve in the kitchen, or some-one that is responsible to clean up after people. That is the wrong mindset. She is a blessing! God has blessed woman and has indeed made her a blessing!

As we go out and make a difference in our world around us, we are reaching the heart of Jesus and serving unto Him. It is our position as women of God and daughters of the King, to give to the poor, to feed the hungry, clothe the naked, and to visit those sick and in prison. Being a blessing and extending the love of Jesus outside of our home is what we are all called to do. As women, we can use our God-given skills to subdue, take dominion and fill the earth with the love and goodness of God simply by reaching out to bring the Gospel to the poor, and demonstrating the love of Jesus.

A woman of God is impacting others and ministering to others as a lifestyle. Her talents are not buried like the lazy servant in Matthew 25:18. But she takes them and multiplies them to further the kingdom of God here on the earth, for eternal purposes.

Some of you might be wondering even now, where do I begin? How do I know what is my God-given calling and specific purpose on this earth? Number one, you are called to glorify God in all you do. You may already know those talents and skills and passions that are deep down inside of your heart. God can take those and use them in a special way to further His kingdom. Everything we do is about making kingdom impact in our world. When we are a godly woman, wife, and mom, we are already making kingdom impact in this world! We are by our example to others and the testimony to them. We also make tremendous impact by the testimony we are to our families and how God is going to use them in this world due to our influence. Even as a single young lady that chooses to serve Jesus and walk in purity, you are making an impact to the young women all around you!

I remember when I came to Bible school in Tampa as a single young woman. I had no idea what God had ultimately called me to do. And it's still unfolding for me. I didn't know I would become a Pastor's wife, or be writing books, doing extended revival meetings, traveling, or preaching in evangelistic crusades. All I knew was that I loved Jesus and I got busy winning souls! If you put souls first, as #1 priority in your pursuit to impact this world, I promise you - every detail of your heart's desires will come to pass. And your gifts and talents and skills will be enhanced and backed up by all of heaven!

Don't let the devil stop you from being a gift to the world! If he can stop you, he can stop the movement of God in the world!! Revival is counting on every man, woman, boy, and girl getting filled and equipped with the fire of God to go and shake nations. You are anointed and appointed for such a time as this! I pray that you are provoked into your destiny to GO and change your world and to be the gift that God has called and ordained you to be! May there be a passion in you sparked like never before, to thrive and to dominate your world!

In Jesus' name. Amen

Workbook Section, Chapter 5:

I would like to utilize this workbook section as a Prayer Journal. Use these pages as a point of contact in your devotion to pray over your husband, your children, and your world and how you can bless them as a daughter of dominion.

1. A Gift to Her Husband:

    a. List desires that you are specifically believing God for with regards to your husband and your marriage.

    _____

    _____

    _____

    _____

    b. What can you do to be more of a blessing to him as his helpmate in helping him to achieve these things?

    _____

    _____

    _____

    _____

2. A Gift to Her Children:

    a. Write below prayer requests that you will go to God for and stand in faith for on behalf of your children:

    _____

    _____

    _____

    _____

b. What daily things can you do as their mom to help them get through this and to become whom God has purposed for them to be?

_____

_____

_____

_____

3. A Gift to Her World:

a. List those things that you are most passionate about?

_____

_____

_____

_____

b. How can you use these things to spread the Gospel of Jesus Christ and be His hands and feet on the earth today?

_____

_____

_____

_____

4. Take some time and pray. PRAY for your husband (or husband to come), pray for your children (or children to come), and pray for your world. Pray for your country, your state, and your city. Pray for your Government Leaders and Pastors and for those that work in your communities. There is power in prayer! And if we've ever needed prayer in our nations, we need it now! Jesus is truly coming soon! Allow God to speak to you even in the quiet and write

down what He speaks to you. God is still speaking on the earth today. We just have to listen. We have to shut down all the noise around us and be still...and listen. When God speaks, His promises are yes and Amen and he always answers by fire! When He speaks, He is going to move!!! Write down what you feel God is saying to you.

Scriptures on Prayer

2 Chronicles 7:14 *"If my people, which are called by my name, shall humble themselves, and pray, and seek my face, and turn from their wicked ways; then will I hear from heaven, and will forgive their sin, and will heal their land."*

Psalms 34:7 *"The righteous cry, and the LORD heareth, and delivereth them out of all their troubles."*

Jeremiah 33:3 *"Call unto me, and I will answer thee, and shew thee great and mighty things, which thou knowest not."*

James 5:16 *"Confess your faults one to another, and pray one for another, that ye may be healed. **The effectual fervent prayer of a righteous man availeth much.**"*

Chapter 6

Becoming a Daughter

W hat does it mean to become a daughter? A daughter is a female offspring of her parents, a descendant, and a product of a particular person, origin or source.

You can become a daughter of God! John 1:11-12 says *"He came unto his own, and his own received him not. But as many as received him, to them he gave the POWER to become the sons of God, even to them that believe on his name."*

> You can become a daughter of God!

Look at some key words. To AS MANY as received Him. There are some people who believe in predestination. This is a whole doctrine that says that the eternal fate of a soul is already prede-termined. This means that God has already chosen who is going to be saved and who isn't. If that's the case, then why would Jesus instruct us to preach the gospel to every creature? Why would we see all throughout God's Word that God gives a choice? We choose either death or life, blessings or cursings. This is not a Jehovah Witnesses religion, where only a pre-selected 144,000 make it into heaven. Absolutely not! There is no limit in heaven and no limit to whose name can be written in the Lambs Book of Life. The Bible says "as many as received him, to them gave he power to become the sons of God." As many is just that - as many. On top of that, The Bible says in 2 Peter 3:9 "The Lord is not slack concerning His promise, as some men count slackness; but is longsuffering to usward, not willing that any should perish, but that ALL should come to repentance."

Then, the Bible says if you receive Him, you will have the POWER to become the sons of God. **This is a powerful adoption!** The natural mind, religion, philosophy, or even science cannot explain it or try to figure it out. No matter who you are, what your race, background, social status, education, past life of sin, it doesn't matter - you can be a child of God! Simply by receiving Him as your Lord and Savior.

> Being a child of God comes with POWER! The same power that raised Christ from the dead dwells in you!

Being a child of God comes with POWER! The same power that raised Christ from the dead dwells in you! (Romans 8:11). And there's a power that works within you that brings *exceedingly and abundantly beyond what we can ask or think"* (Ephesians 3:20). There's a dunamis power (God's distinct power) that you can receive as a child of God when the Holy Ghost comes upon you! (Acts 1:8)

Revelation of this power activates it into your life and you can begin walking in the supernatural.

A son is a son or a daughter. In Christ, we are spirit beings created equally in His image and there is neither male nor female, Jew nor Greek, bond nor free. He sees us all in the spirit, as spirit beings. The Bible says we are "all one in Christ Jesus" (Galatians 3:28-29). So, the term "sons" here is referring to both sons and daughters.

As a daughter of God, you are His offspring, descendant and a product of Himself and all that He entails. As a natural daughter, I'm sure you can think right now of all the ways that you resemble your earthly father - physically, mentally, emotionally, and in character and giftings. If God is all knowing, all powerful, Creator of all the Universe in just 7 days, then just take a moment to think that YOU are HIS daughter and those very traits and character qualities are now IN YOU! There's been a powerful exchange of the old you to

> Everything in Heaven is rightfully yours. Every quality that God has is now yours!

the new you, in your NEW BIRTH to be a daughter of the King of Kings and the Lord of Lords. Everything in Heaven is rightfully yours. Every quality that God has is now yours! Creativity, Wisdom, Authority in Heaven, Holiness, Powerful, every attribute! Hallelujah! And as a matter of fact, anything you desire all you have to do is to ask your Abba Father for it and He will give it to you.

Look at Matthew 7:7-11:

> *Ask, and it shall be given you; seek, and ye shall find; knock, and it shall be opened unto you:*
>
> *For every one that asketh receiveth; and he that seeketh findeth; and to him that knocketh it shall be opened.*
>
> *Or what man is there of you, whom if his son ask bread, will he give him a stone?*
>
> *Or if he ask a fish, will he give him a serpent?*
>
> *If ye then, being evil, know how to give good gifts unto your children, how much more shall your Father which is in heaven give good things to them that ask him?*

When you are adopted as a daughter of God, there is freedom and deliverance for you. Let's look at some key stories in the Word of God and how God extends an open door for anyone and everyone to receive adoption, no matter their past or circumstance.

Woman with the infirmity

Luke 13:10-17

> *And he was teaching in one of the synagogues on the sabbath.*
>
> *And, behold, there was a woman which had a spirit of infirmity eighteen years, and was bowed together, and could in no wise lift up herself.*
>
> *And when Jesus saw her, he called her to him, and said unto her, Woman, thou art loosed from thine infirmity.*
>
> *And he laid his hands on her: and immediately she was made straight, and glorified God.*
>
> *And the ruler of the synagogue answered with indignation, because that Jesus healed on the sabbath days, and said unto the people, There are six days in which men ought to work: in them therefore come and be healed and not on the sabbath day.*
>
> *The Lord then answered him, and said, Thou hypocrite, doth not each one of you on the sabbath, loose his ox or his ass from the stall, and lead him away to watering?*
>
> *And ought not this woman, being a daughter of Abraham, whom Satan hath bound, lo, these eighteen years, be loosed from this bond on the sabbath day?*
>
> *And when he had said these things, all his adversaries were ashamed, and all the people rejoiced for all the glorious things that were done by him.*

We can see here that this woman was a daughter of Abraham. She had an infirmity in her body, a spirit that bound her body and bent her over for 18 years. It had taken her over to the point that she couldn't even stand straight and lift herself from bending to the ground. When Jesus saw her, He loosed her from the infirmity, and she was healed immediately. This woman then glorified God! Religion points out the law and that Jesus healed on the

Sabbath and totally negates the fact that she once was bound but now she is free. Religion is bondage. It puts traditions and rules over the presence of God. Religion would rather have a woman bound with infirmity for 18 years and have to wait to be healed on a certain day of the week. Religion would say that you can't pray for the sick or lay hands on a

> Thank God Jesus came on the scene and He is now Lord of the Sabbath!!

person due to the "social distancing" rule because of a virus. But sister, this person is getting FREE! Thank God Jesus came on the scene and He is now Lord of the Sabbath!!

Matthew 12:8 *"For the Son of man is Lord even of the sabbath day."*

Even as a daughter, many don't even realize the power living on the inside of them and that they have authority over sickness and disease. Thank God for His goodness and grace and mercy, that Jesus came on the scene and in one touch, the anointing broke her yoke of bondage!

She was a daughter that received the privileges that come with being a daughter of the King of Kings, Jehovah-Rapha, the Lord who heals us.

Woman caught in the act of adultery

John 8:1-11

Jesus went unto the mount of Olives.

And early in the morning he came again into the temple, and all the people came unto him; and he sat down, and taught them.

And the scribes and Pharisees brought unto him a woman taken in adultery; and when they had set her in the midst,

They say unto him, Master, this woman was taken in adultery, in the very act.

Now Moses in the law commanded us, that such should be stoned: but what sayest thou?

This they said, tempting him, that they might have to accuse him. But Jesus stooped down, and with his finger wrote on the ground, as though he heard them not.

So when they continued asking him, he lifted up himself, and said unto them, He that is without sin among you, let him first cast a stone at her.

And again he stooped down, and wrote on the ground.

And they which heard it, being convicted by their own conscience, went out one by one, beginning at the eldest, even unto the last: and Jesus was left alone, and the woman standing in the midst.

When Jesus had lifted up himself, and saw none but the woman, he said unto her, Woman, where are those thine accusers? hath no man condemned thee?

She said, No man, Lord. And Jesus said unto her, Neither do I condemn thee: go, and sin no more.

This woman has a circumstance that she is facing and it is life or death. She is about to be killed due to her sin. Then Jesus steps on the scene and defends her and covers her with his forgiveness and mercy. He runs off all of her accusers, and she faces the Lord alone. This is how I imagined my own life once all the naysayers and accusers and mockers were out of the picture and I sat alone in my parent's basement. When all those who

> When all those who laughed at, judged, and ridiculed you have been removed, you can stand openly before your Creator, the One who is longing for your attention.

laughed at, judged, and ridiculed you have been removed, you can stand openly before your Creator, the One who is longing for your attention.

When you get alone with God, He is saying "I don't condemn you! I just want you to go, be free, and sin no more. I want you to live righteously because you can! Because now you have the power to! This is not going to be something you'll figure out how to do on your own before you come to Me! No! You have a one on one encounter with Me first and THEN you will have the power to sin no more! The plan that I have for your life is greater than this! You were not born or created to be an adulterer! But to be a daughter!" Jesus is calling! And He is saying, "Go in freedom and do my will. You are totally free now because you got alone with Me. And allowed me to get into the secret closet that you wouldn't allow anyone else to get into."

> The plan that I have for your life is greater than this! You were not born or created to be an adulterer! But to be a daughter!

There are people that need to be removed from your life because all they do is remind you about your past, the things you used to do, the person you used to be. But when you are in Christ, and you walk after the spirit and not after the flesh, the Bible says there is no condemnation to you (Romans 8:1). When those people go, you can see and hear clearly from God and you will be totally free from your past. There are deliverance blockers out there, literally on an assignment from the enemy to keep you bound.

Woman at the well

John 4:5-29

> *Then cometh he to a city of Samaria, which is called Sychar, near to the parcel of ground that Jacob gave to his son Joseph.*

Now Jacob's well was there. Jesus therefore, being wearied with his journey, sat thus on the well: and it was about the sixth hour.

There cometh a woman of Samaria to draw water: Jesus saith unto her, Give me to drink.

(For his disciples were gone away unto the city to buy meat.)

Then saith the woman of Samaria unto him, How is it that thou, being a Jew, askest drink of me, which am a woman of Samaria? for the Jews have no dealings with the Samaritans.

Jesus answered and said unto her, If thou knewest the gift of God, and who it is that saith to thee, Give me to drink; thou wouldest have asked of him, and he would have given thee living water.

The woman saith unto him, Sir, thou hast nothing to draw with, and the well is deep: from whence then hast thou that living water?

Art thou greater than our father Jacob, which gave us the well, and drank thereof himself, and his children, and his cattle?

Jesus answered and said unto her, Whosoever drinketh of this water shall thirst again:

But whosoever drinketh of the water that I shall give him shall never thirst; but the water that I shall give him shall be in him a well of water springing up into everlasting life.

The woman saith unto him, Sir, give me this water, that I thirst not, neither come hither to draw.

Jesus saith unto her, Go, call thy husband, and come hither.

The woman answered and said, I have no husband. Jesus said unto her, Thou hast well said, I have no husband:

For thou hast had five husbands; and he whom thou now hast is not thy husband: in that saidst thou truly.

The woman saith unto him, Sir, I perceive that thou art a prophet.

Our fathers worshipped in this mountain; and ye say, that in Jerusalem is the place where men ought to worship.

Jesus saith unto her, Woman, believe me, the hour cometh, when ye shall neither in this mountain, nor yet at Jerusalem, worship the Father.

Ye worship ye know not what: we know what we worship: for salvation is of the Jews.

But the hour cometh, and now is, when the true worshippers shall worship the Father in spirit and in truth: for the Father seeketh such to worship him.

God is a Spirit: and they that worship him must worship him in spirit and in truth.

The woman saith unto him, I know that Messias cometh, which is called Christ: when he is come, he will tell us all things.

Jesus saith unto her, I that speak unto thee am he.

And upon this came his disciples, and marvelled that he talked with the woman: yet no man said, What seekest thou? or, Why talkest thou with her?

The woman then left her waterpot, and went her way into the city, and saith to the men,

Come, see a man, which told me all things that ever I did: is not this the Christ?

You can see here this woman went from having 5 husbands and living with a man who she was not married to, to now she is proclaiming the news of Christ the Messiah across Samaria. It didn't matter to Jesus what her past was. She could have been married 15 times or have been a prostitute, Jesus turned NO ONE away that came to Him or encountered Him. It doesn't matter if you have been divorced 6 times, or have 5 kids by 5 different men, you can still be a daughter of the King. This woman was hungry for a drink of the Living Water and I believe that every

> Jesus turned NO ONE away that came to Him or encountered Him.

time she came back to that well to draw water she was reminded of her encounter with Jesus. A man that knew everything about her but yet loved her enough to break the custom and the law of a Jew talking with a Samaritan woman and ministering to her. This was also the longest recorded conversation in the Bible that Jesus had with any one person. She asked for a drink of the living water! She believed there was a Messiah coming and Jesus told her it was indeed Him. She then left her waterpot to share the news! This woman believed! She was a preacher of this Good News! I believe she became a daughter!

The Gentile Woman

Mark 7:24-30

> And from thence he arose, and went into the borders of Tyre and Sidon, and entered into an house, and would have no man know it: but he could not be hid.
>
> For a certain woman, whose young daughter had an unclean spirit, heard of him, and came and fell at his feet:
>
> The woman was a Greek, a Syrophenician by nation; and she besought him that he would cast forth the devil out of her daughter.
>
> But Jesus said unto her, Let the children first be filled: for it is not meet to take the children's bread, and to cast it unto the dogs.

And she answered and said unto him, Yes, Lord: yet the dogs under the table eat of the children's crumbs.

And he said unto her, For this saying go thy way; the devil is gone out of thy daughter.

And when she was come to her house, she found the devil gone out, and her daughter laid upon the bed.

We see here a woman that was a Greek. She came to a Jewish man, which was out of custom and against the law. She needed a miracle! Her daughter was possessed with a devil. But Jesus said, "Let the children first be filled: for it is not meet to take the children's bread, and to cast it unto the dogs." This is because salvation was for the Jews and it was not yet offered to the Gentiles. This woman was fearless and also relentless in her faith. She did not allow an offense to stand in the way of the miracle she so desperately needed for her daughter. She responds, *"Yes Lord: yet the dogs under the table eat of the children's crumbs."* She knew that even in a crumb from the children's bread, she could receive her miracle. Jesus said He is the Bread of Life. This

> This woman was fearless and also relentless in her faith. She did not allow an offense to stand in the way of the miracle she so desperately needed for her daughter.

bread (His body) is our Communion and has the healing power to drive out sickness. Just one touch, one taste, one crumb of this bread can bring supernatural miracles into your body! Her faith was prophetic of the Crucifixion and Resurrection to come and the healing power that would come forth from the body of Jesus. Her faith overlooked her feelings and offense. Her faith overlooked her right to close the door of Jesus on her entire generation of Gentiles. Instead, her faith moved Jesus to give her the miracle she needed! This woman was desperate for her daughter to be delivered. Her desperation opened the door to generations to have faith in Jesus, as their Savior and as their Healer. It doesn't matter if you are Jew or a Gentile, saved or unsaved, male or female, rich or poor. Social status, race, gender, popularity, none of it matters in the kingdom to God. Jesus didn't come to save a particular skin color, He came to save the souls of the world!! You can be a "dog" of society, the lowest of low, and Jesus still cares. He went to the Cross for the entire world. Jesus is ready and willing to heal you, save you, set you free, and give you the very miracle that you need. Only believe!

> Jesus didn't come to save a particular skin color. He came to save the souls of the world!!

Romans 2:10-11 *"But glory, honour, and peace, to every man that worketh good, to the Jew first, and also to the Gentile. 11 For there is no respect of persons with God."*

Romans 1:16 *"For I am not ashamed of the gospel of Christ: for it is the power of God unto salvation to every one that believeth; to the Jew first, and also to the Greek."*

Acts 28:28 *"Be it known therefore unto you, that the salvation of God is sent unto the Gentiles, and that they will hear it."*

Acts 10:34-48

Then Peter opened his mouth, and said, Of a truth I perceive that God is no respecter of persons:

But in every nation he that feareth him, and worketh righteousness, is accepted with him.

The word which God sent unto the children of Israel, preaching peace by Jesus Christ: (he is Lord of all:)

That word, I say, ye know, which was published through-out all Judaea, and began from Galilee, after the baptism which John preached;

How God anointed Jesus of Nazareth with the Holy Ghost and with power: who went about doing good, and healing all that were oppressed of the devil; for God was with him.

And we are witnesses of all things which he did both in the land of the Jews, and in Jerusalem; whom they slew and hanged on a tree:

Him God raised up the third day, and shewed him openly;

Not to all the people, but unto witnesses chosen before God, even to us, who did eat and drink with him after he rose from the dead.

And he commanded us to preach unto the people, and to testify that it is he which was ordained of God to be the Judge of quick and dead.

*To him give all the prophets witness, that through his name **whosoever** believeth in him shall receive remission of sins.*

*While Peter yet spake these words, the Holy Ghost fell on **all** them which heard the word.*

*And they of the circumcision which believed were aston-ished, as many as came with Peter, because that **on the Gentiles also was poured out the gift of the Holy Ghost.***

For they heard them speak with tongues, and magnify God. Then answered Peter,

Can any man forbid water, that these should not be bap-tized, which have received the Holy Ghost as well as we?

And he commanded them to be baptized in the name of the Lord. Then prayed they him to tarry certain days.

Peter was given a detailed dream that totally and completely demonstrates the love of Jesus and His redemptive power available to the entire world. He told Peter in Acts 10 to rise and not to call that which God has cleansed common or unclean. God called Cornelius, a Roman Centurion (Gentile) in a vision to go directly to Peter to receive direction and answers to his prayers before the Lord. When Cornelius encountered Peter, Peter knew that this was due to his dream and knew the interpretation of exactly what God was showing him. He begins to speak in verse 24. And we see in verse 44, that while Peter spoke the words of the Truth and the Gospel, the Holy Ghost fell upon the Gentiles and they got baptized also in water!

Woman with the issue of blood

Mark 5:25-34

And a certain woman, which had an issue of blood twelve years,

And had suffered many things of many physicians, and had spent all that she had, and was nothing bettered, but rather grew worse,

When she had heard of Jesus, came in the press behind, and touched his garment.

For she said, If I may touch but his clothes, I shall be whole.

And straightway the fountain of her blood was dried up; and she felt in her body that she was healed of that plague.

And Jesus, immediately knowing in himself that virtue had gone out of him, turned him about in the press, and said, Who touched my clothes?

And his disciples said unto him, Thou seest the multitude thronging thee, and sayest thou, Who touched me?

And he looked round about to see her that had done this thing.

But the woman fearing and trembling, knowing what was done in her, came and fell down before him, and told him all the truth.

And he said unto her, Daughter, thy faith hath made thee whole; go in peace, and be whole of thy plague.

In Luke Chapter 8 we can find this same story. When she touched Him, Jesus said in verse 46: "Somebody hath touched me." You can see in this passage that this woman went from a certain woman, to a somebody, to a DAUGHTER! All because of her FAITH. Because she humbled herself and came bowing before Him. She was adopted into the family of believers. Salvation and redemption came to her. She was an heir according to the promise of Abraham! Her desperation made room for her.

> This woman went from a certain woman, to a somebody, to a DAUGHTER!

I'm here to testify that God will take you from a nobody to a somebody, from an orphan to a daughter, from a condition to a position, from grass to grace, from zero to shero! If God created the entire Universe in 7 days, He can give you your miracle in a split of a second! God wrote your story and He will finish it! Your latter shall be greater!

This woman had an "issue" of blood. Maybe an issue of blood isn't your exact issue. It could be an issue of the mind, an issue of the heart, an issue in your physical body - whatever it may be, just give it to Jesus. Be truthful with Him. He already knows the truth anyways. I'm here to tell you that Jesus is ready and willing and perfectly able to touch you today with His healing and delivering FIRE POWER.

You can become a Daughter even right now and by faith be completely whole! Completely healed in your body and set free from all pain and destruction. Hallelujah! Psalm 107:20 states: *"He sends forth His word and heals them and rescues them from the pit and destruction."*

1. What are some of the natural birth rights that you have received from your own 2 parents?

_____

_____

_____

_____

_____

_____

_____

2. What are some of the birthrights that you have inherited as a child of God?

_____

_____

_____

_____

_____

_____

_____

3. What has your heavenly Father done for you that an earthly Father could never achieve?

_____

_____

_____

_____

_____

_____

_____

_____

4. What woman in this Chapter do you feel your testimony relates to the most and why?

_____

_____

_____

_____

_____

_____

_____

_____

5. How does it feel to be a daughter of King Jesus?

_____

_____

_____

_____

_____

_____

_____

_____

_____

Chapter 7

God's Covenant

G od has established an all embracing binding relationship (covenant) with his creation. We will discuss in this chapter what a Covenant is and how it relates to us today, as children of God. So then, what is a Covenant? I'm glad you asked. A Covenant is a binding contract or agreement between two parties. In the Old Testament, the Hebrew word "berith" is used. Berith is derived from a root which means "to cut", and hence a covenant is a "cutting", with reference to cutting or dividing of animals into two parts, and the contracting parties passion between them in making a covenant (Genesis 15; Jeremiah 34:18-19). In the New Testament, the word for Covenant is Greek word "diatheke", which carries the same meaning but speaks of a New Covenant and a better way. We have the Old Covenant and we have the New Covenant. We move from a Covenant of works to a Covenant of Grace.

In the New Covenant we have a Covenant of Grace - the eternal plan of redemption entered into by the three Persons of the Godhead, and carried out and completed in its fullness. Jesus Christ, comes as the second Adam (to complete what the first Adam could not do), representing all his people, assuming their place and undertaking all their obligations under the violated covenant of works. *"For by grace are ye saved through faith; and that not of yourselves: it is the gift of God: Not of works, lest any man should boast."* Ephesians 2:8-9

In the Old Testament, under the Law, the people would have to confess their sins to the High Priest and once a year he would offer sacrifices for them and himself on the Day of Atonement. The blood of animals was shed to cover their sins.

(See Leviticus 17:11) *"For the life of the flesh is in the blood: and I have given it to you upon the altar to make an atonement for your souls: for it is the blood that maketh an atonement for the soul."*

A scapegoat would be sent as far as the east was from the west (2 sent out in total opposite directions) to represent the people being pardoned for their trespasses. There was no direct access to God and the shedding of animals' blood was made for remission of their sins. I cannot even imagine having to carry the burden of my sin for 364 days to that one day each year where sacrifice of blood was made in order for me to be forgiven. What a glorious Covenant we do not live in!

At the atonement, Jesus shed His blood for the sins of all humanity. And when He died He went down into hell to take the keys of death, hell and the grave. The Bible says He spoiled every principality and made a show of them openly, triumphing over them in it (Colossians 2:15). The veil of the temple was torn into 2. No longer did man have to stand on the outer courts of the temple. But man had direct access to God, into the Holy of Holies - into the anointing and the presence of God to speak to Him directly and not through a man. No longer did animals have to be sacrificed for the sins of the people. Because the Ultimate Sacrifice, the Ultimate Lamb gave His life on that wooden cross for you and for me.

Look at Hebrews Chapter 8:

Now of the things which we have spoken this is the sum: We have such an high priest, who is set on the right hand of the throne of the Majesty in the heavens;

A minister of the sanctuary, and of the true tabernacle, which the Lord pitched, and not man.

For every high priest is ordained to offer gifts and sacrifices: wherefore it is of necessity that this man have somewhat also to offer.

For if he were on earth, he should not be a priest, seeing that there are priests that offer gifts according to the law:

Who serve unto the example and shadow of heavenly things, as Moses was admonished of God when he was about to make the tabernacle: for, See, saith he, that thou make all things according to the pattern shewed to thee in the mount.

But now hath he obtained a more excellent ministry, by how much also he is the mediator of a better covenant, which was established upon better promises.

For if that first covenant had been faultless, then should no place have been sought for the second.

For finding fault with them, he saith, Behold, the days come, saith the Lord, when I will make a new covenant with the house of Israel and with the house of Judah:

Not according to the covenant that I made with their fathers in the day when I took them by the hand to lead them out of the land of Egypt; because they continued not in my covenant, and I regarded them not, saith the Lord.

For this is the covenant that I will make with the house of Israel after those days, saith the Lord; I will put my laws into their mind, and write them in their hearts: and I will be to them a God, and they shall be to me a people:

And they shall not teach every man his neighbour, and every man his brother, saying, Know the Lord: for all shall know me, from the least to the greatest.

For I will be merciful to their unrighteousness, and their sins and their iniquities will I remember no more.

In that he saith, A new covenant, he hath made the first old. Now that which decayeth and waxeth old is ready to vanish away.

The first Covenant failed with Adam. When Adam fell in the Garden of Eden, God knew that He had to send another to re-establish His eternal Covenant with man. Christ, the Mediator of both Testaments/ Covenants, fulfills all its conditions on behalf of His people, and dispenses to them all its blessings. This is why the seed of Jesus was so important - without Him, we would be in a lost eternity, our souls damned forever. We would be dead spiritually and in neverending torment in fire that is never quenched. Jesus is the 2nd Adam, the One who would and DID destroy the enemy once and for all.

> Jesus is the 2nd Adam, the One who would and DID destroy the enemy once and for all.

Look at Hebrews Chapter 9:

Then verily the first covenant had also ordinances of divine service, and a worldly sanctuary.

For there was a tabernacle made; the first, wherein was the candlestick, and the table, and the shewbread; which is called the sanctuary.

And after the second veil, the tabernacle which is called the Holiest of all;

Which had the golden censer, and the ark of the covenant overlaid round about with gold, wherein was the golden pot that had manna, and Aaron's rod that budded, and the tables of the covenant;

And over it the cherubims of glory shadowing the mercy seat; of which we cannot now speak particularly.

Now when these things were thus ordained, the priests went always into the first tabernacle, accomplishing the service of God.

But into the second went the high priest alone once every year, not without blood, which he offered for himself, and for the errors of the people:

The Holy Ghost this signifying, that the way into the holiest of all was not yet made manifest, while as the first tabernacle was yet standing:

Which was a figure for the time then present, in which were offered both gifts and sacrifices, that could not make him that did the service perfect, as pertaining to the conscience;

Which stood only in meats and drinks, and divers washings, and carnal ordinances, imposed on them until the time of reformation.

But Christ being come an high priest of good things to come, by a greater and more perfect tabernacle, not made with hands, that is to say, not of this building;

Neither by the blood of goats and calves, but by his own blood he entered in once into the holy place, having obtained eternal redemption for us.

For if the blood of bulls and of goats, and the ashes of an heifer sprinkling the unclean, sanctifieth to the purifying of the flesh:

How much more shall the blood of Christ, who through the eternal Spirit offered himself without spot to God, purge your conscience from dead works to serve the living God?

And for this cause he is the mediator of the new testament, that by means of death, for the redemption of the transgressions that were under the first testament, they which are called might receive the promise of eternal inheritance.

For where a testament is, there must also of necessity be the death of the testator.

For a testament is of force after men are dead: otherwise it is of no strength at all while the testator liveth.

Whereupon neither the first testament was dedicated without blood.

For when Moses had spoken every precept to all the people according to the law, he took the blood of calves and of goats, with water, and scarlet wool, and hyssop, and sprinkled both the book, and all the people,

Saying, This is the blood of the testament which God hath enjoined unto you.

Moreover he sprinkled with blood both the tabernacle, and all the vessels of the ministry.

*And almost all things are by the law purged with blood; and **without shedding of blood is no remission.***

It was therefore necessary that the patterns of things in the heavens should be purified with these; but the heavenly things themselves with better sacrifices than these.

For Christ is not entered into the holy places made with hands, which are the figures of the true; but into heaven itself, now to appear in the presence of God for us:

Nor yet that he should offer himself often, as the high priest entereth into the holy place every year with blood of others;

For then must he often have suffered since the foundation of the world: but now once in the end of the world hath he appeared to put away sin by the sacrifice of himself.

And as it is appointed unto men once to die, but after this the judgment:

So Christ was once offered to bear the sins of many; and unto them that look for him shall he appear the second time without sin unto salvation.

My goodness, Read that again! If the blood of bulls and goats can cleanse you, God is saying - How much more can the blood of Christ cleanse you! The lamb without spot or blemish, can so much greater purge your conscience from dead works to serve the living God!

So as you can see now, the New Testament has perfected the Old Testament. It completed it and made it possible through the grace of our Lord and Savior. Through His atonement, complete forgiveness of sins is achieved. There is a new bold access to God achieved that was not available in the Old Testament. Hebrews 4:16 says *"Let us therefore come boldly unto the throne of grace, that we may obtain mercy, and find grace to help in time of need."* Grace is God's supernatural

> The New Testament has perfected the Old Testament. It completed it and made it possible through the grace of our Lord and Savior.

ability in you, to do that which you cannot do in and of yourself. It is truly God's unmerited favor upon His children!

God's Old Covenant was written and established in the book of Exodus chapter 20 with the Ten Commandments. When we go to Genesis chapter 9, God also gave His covenant to Noah that He would never again flood the earth. In Genesis 17, God told Abraham that he would be a father of many nations and be exceeding fruitful with nations made from him and the land of Canaan. When we read Deuteronomy 28, we see that God made a Covenant with the children of Israel. He promised that He would bless them and give them the land which He promised them. The condition for them was that they would hearken diligently to His Word and obey His commandments. Every one of these Covenants belong to us. They still stand in effect! His covenants are EVERLASTING!

Psalm 103:17-18

"But the mercy of the Lord is from everlasting to everlasting upon them that fear him, and his righteousness unto children's children; To such as keep his covenant, and to those that remember his commandments to do them."

His eternal Covenant is for the righteous and to all their generations.

Some folks have said that the Old Covenant has passed away. But it is there for a reason! The Old Covenant isn't old and void and eradicated. It is because of the New Covenant that it is now POSSIBLE! It's possible to attain, possible to keep, possible to follow and possible to receive by grace and by faith!! With God's Covenants, all we have to do is to fulfill our end of the Covenant. A Covenant takes action on the part of both parties involved and in the Covenant. Being a joint heir of a Covenant is simple. If we keep His commands, He will prosper us and fulfill His end of the Covenant.

> The Old Covenant isn't old and void and eradicated. It is because of the New Covenant that it is now POSSIBLE!

If we obey God's covenant, we can receive the blessings from it. IF we accept Him as Lord & Savior into our lives, then we can accept His blessings, and protection, and favor. Obedience always yields rewards and the fruit of it's requirement.

In Matthew 5, Jesus invalidates this conclusion that the Old Covenant has died or is irrelevant. This is just a couple of the many examples in the New Covenant:

Matthew 5:19-22

Whosoever therefore shall break one of these least commandments, and shall teach men so, he shall be called the least in the kingdom of heaven: but whosoever shall do and teach them, the same shall be called great in the kingdom of heaven.

For I say unto you, That except your righteousness shall exceed the righteousness of the scribes and Pharisees, ye shall in no case enter into the kingdom of heaven.

Ye have heard that it was said of them of old time, Thou shalt not kill; and whosoever shall kill shall be in danger of the judgment:

But I say unto you, That whosoever is angry with his brother without a cause shall be in danger of the judgment: and whosoever shall say to his brother, Raca, shall be in danger of the council: but whosoever shall say, Thou fool, shall be in danger of hell fire.

You see, in the Law, it was said under the Old Covenant that we are not to murder. But Jesus says if you hate your brother or if you call him "Raca", interpreted "empty headed fool", then you are in danger of hell fire. Hey, I didn't say it, Jesus said it!

Now, look at verses 27-28:

Ye have heard that it was said by them of old time, Thou shalt not commit adultery:

But I say unto you, That whosoever looketh on a woman to lust after her hath committed adultery with her already in his heart.

So, in the New Testament, not only is the standard remaining that we are commanded not to commit adultery. But Jesus takes it a step further and says that if you look after a person with lust then you have already committed adultery in your heart.

Some people even argue that tithing is under the Law. If you don't believe in tithing, you are literally bound to poverty and separated from the covenant of God. You don't have to tithe and God does not have to bless you. He does not have to open the windows of heaven over your life and the nations do not have to call you blessed. Abraham paid tithes to the high priest Melchizedek before the Law was even established (Genesis 14:20; Hebrews 7).

In the Old Covenant, a tenth was required. But we can even see in the New Testament, not only did a widow bring her last 2 mites, but we see Mary of Bethany pouring her alabaster box of a year's salary and wages and pouring it on the Master's feet! If the Old Covenant required 10% then surely the New Covenant requires our all!

Lastly, read Matthew 22:35-40:

> *Then one of them, which was a lawyer, asked him a question, tempting him, and saying,*
>
> *Master, which is the great commandment in the law?*
>
> *Jesus said unto him, Thou shalt love the Lord thy God with all thy heart, and with all thy soul, and with all thy mind.*
>
> *This is the first and great commandment.*
>
> *And the second is like unto it, Thou shalt love thy neighbour as thyself.*
>
> *On these two commandments hang all the law and the prophets.*

All 613 laws of the Old Covenant, Jesus sums up in these 2. If we put Jesus first, loving Him with everything in us, then we can love ourselves enough to love our neighbor equally. When we do this, keeping His laws and commands becomes easy!

You and I being in the New Covenant, have not only the blood of Jesus which made a way for us to come directly to Him, but we also have the awesome Holy Spirit that will help us to establish His Covenant here on the earth. We truly have everything we need available to us in God's Word from beginning to end. There is absolutely nothing missing, nothing lacking, and nothing broken.

1. Jesus gave us the Greatest 2 commandments: To love the Lord thy God with all of our heart, soul, and mind. And to love our neighbor as ourselves. Let's journal some things here that you will do this week to make adjustments and develop the priority of these 2 commandments in our lives.

    a. Love the Lord with all of our hearts, minds, and souls. When we make God #1 and have no other gods before Him, we can achieve this commandment. Nothing in this world can separate us from the love of God. Our souls long for more of Him and we seek Him early, and with everything in us. **What are some steps that you will incorporate into your daily routine to put God first and make Him #1?**

    _____

    _____

    _____

    _____

    _____

    _____

    b. Love our neighbor. Souls are the currency of heaven. What we do for others, we do for Jesus. Loving your neighbor is not just loving your friends, or loving people that look like you or talk like you. It is loving people just because they are God's creation and because He loves them. Everyone is your neighbor: the drunk man depressed at the bar, the homeless lady with a cup of coins, the rich man smoking a pipe, and the mom walking her child in a wheelchair - it doesn't matter. You can be a blessing! God promised Abraham in a covenant with him "And I will make of thee a great nation, and I will bless thee, and make thy name great; and thou shalt be a blessing." Genesis 12:2. God will not only bless you but also make you a blessing! You are blessed not just because God loves you and you are His daughter but because He also wants you to BE a blessing! What are 2 things you will commit to doing this week to love your neighbor and be a blessing?

_____

_____

_____

_____

_____

c. The Bible says that we are to love our neighbor **as our own selves**. This means, we are to actually love US for who God made us to be. We have to love who we are, forgive ourselves, value and appreciate ourselves. We actually have to take care of and bless ourselves. Edify yourself in prayer, build yourself up in faith, strengthen your inner man, clothe yourself in strength and dignity. Speak over every part of you and bless your body with health and strength and long life. **What can you do this week to demonstrate love for yourself?** _

_____

_____

_____

_____

_____

d. **Look in the mirror, hug yourself and say "You are loved!"**

Chapter 8

Take Dominion, Daughter

$\mathcal{D}$aughter of the Almighty God, you have an opportunity to demonstrate His power on the earth today! When God told us to be fruitful, multiply, replenish, subdue the earth and have dominion - He meant it! To take dominion means to take authority and to take possession, to flourish and to "reign as kings and priests" on this earth! (Rev 1:6)

I believe we are in a time and in an hour that God is going to use women like never before! He is raising up women evangelists and revivalists to do things that have never been done before. Kathryn Kuhlman was great, Amiee Semple McPhearson was amazing. But you know what, they aren't here anymore, YOU are! I'm talking about a wave of women that won't compromise, that won't settle or live in mediocrity, that won't conform to this world! A woman set apart, consecrated for the glory of God! Walking in raw Book of Acts power! Baptized in the Holy Ghost and fire! Not afraid of what man or religion or government can do to her. Her main concern is pleasing God and living for eternity. I'm talking about a woman that has counted the cost and has already lost her life in Christ. She is willing to pay the price to do whatever it takes to take dominion and turn the world upside down for Jesus! We, as daughters, are anointed, appointed, and equipped. We are women of exploits, walking in strong gifts of power. It is our rightful inheritance and we take it boldly.

> There's a word in your spirit, there's a message in your belly! You are pregnant with something huge and now the date of deliverance has come!

There's a word in your spirit, there's a message in your belly! You are pregnant with something huge and now the date of deliverance has come! It's time for the baby to come forth and be released in the world.

There are 4 Keys to Taking Dominion that we will cover:

1. Renew your mind with the Word of God.

You first have to change your mindset. Make up your mind. You either are living in faith or you are living in fear. You are a Victor and not a victim! You are above only and never beneath! The head and not the tail! You are not conquered, but you are a conqueror! Don't make any excuses and stop looking down on yourself. Thanks to the blood of Jesus you haven't come too short for God to use you. You haven't missed the mark! You are right on time and right on target. God can redeem your past. God has divinely set you up to take dominion in this time and in this hour. You are not too young, you are not too old. You are not too thin, too thick, too rich or too poor! Your past did not disqualify you! It qualified you for your future! A great man of God once said, "God doesn't call the qualified. He qualifies the called."

Look at 2 Corinthians 10:4-5 *"For the weapons of our warfare are not carnal, but mighty through God to the pulling down of strong holds; casting down imaginations, and every high thing that exalteth itself against the knowledge of God, and bringing into captivity every thought to the obedience of Christ."* This scripture set me free in my times of pregnancy when the enemy was lying to me and trying to put fear in me. He sends fiery darts to try to stop you and you literally have to cast them down! Rebuke them! Don't accept them. And bring those thoughts captive with the Word of God. Whatever the devil is telling you, contradict it with the WORD. That's exactly how Jesus overcame him when He told him "It is written."

One of the biggest areas most Christian women I've seen needed to get delivered in, is from their own minds! Sometimes, the devil doesn't even have any work to do because people are a victim to their own minds. They are constantly battling fear, doubt, worry, you name it. Literally, if you can train your mind to only think on GOOD things (Philipians 4:8) you will shock yourself on how free you feel and the potential within you!

> if you can train your mind to only think on GOOD things (Philipians 4:8) you will shock yourself on how free you feel and the potential within you!

The Bible says to occupy until he comes (Luke 19:13). Not sit around and watch Netflix or Desperate Housewives. But to go into all the world and preach the Gospel. To lay hands on the sick - go to the hospitals, the prisons, to the sick and shut in, the homeless shelters, and the abused women's shelters....and bring revival! His word is a hammer that breaks the rock into pieces! You carry the anointing of God! It is there to break and destroy every yoke of bondage and affliction! What does God's Word say about you? Write it on the tablet of your heart. Know your authority in Christ and take action! Ephesians 2:6 *"And hath raised us up together, and made us sit together in heavenly places in Christ Jesus."*

2. Get Consecrated

You have to take dominion over the flesh. When you consecrate yourself, sin and things that choke your time can't continue. When you are in total consecration, you can be a vessel of power for God's glory. Let's go to Romans 12:1. It says, *I beseech you therefore, brethren, by the mercies of God, that ye present your bodies a living sacrifice, holy, acceptable unto God, which is your reasonable service.*

Paul was talking to the Church. They had already given their souls to God, now their bodies had to follow.

1 Corinthians 6:9-20 *"Know ye not that the unrighteous shall not inherit the kingdom of God? Be not deceived: neither fornicators, nor idolaters, nor adulterers, nor effeminate, nor abusers of themselves with mankind, Nor thieves, nor covetous, nor drunkards, nor revilers, nor extortioners, shall inherit the kingdom of God. And such were some of you: but ye are washed, but ye are sanctified, but ye are justified in the name of the Lord Jesus, and by the Spirit of our God. All things are lawful unto me, but all things are not expedient: all things are lawful for me, but I will not be brought under the power of any. Meats for the belly, and the belly for meats: but God shall destroy both it and them. Now the body is not for fornication, but for the Lord; and the Lord for the body. And God hath both raised up the Lord, and will also raise up us by his own power. Know ye not that your bodies are the members of Christ? shall I then take the members of Christ, and make them the members of an harlot? God forbid. What? know ye not that he which is joined to an harlot is one body? for two, saith he, shall be one flesh. But he that is joined unto the Lord is one spirit. Flee fornication. Every sin that a man doeth is without the body; but he that committeth fornication sinneth against his own body. What? know ye not that your body is the temple of the Holy Ghost which is in you, which ye have of God, and ye are not your own? For ye are bought with a price: therefore glorify God in your body, and in your spirit, which are God's.*

There is a standard of holiness that has to come forward in this hour! Consecration will completely free you from a life of sin and empty you of the past.

What is consecration? The definition in Wikipedia says, the solemn dedication to a special purpose or service. Associated with "sacred" or to "sanctify". We are going to go a little bit deeper.

It's a divine separation from the things of the world in exchange for a permanent connection to the things of God.

It's total, absolute, unconditional, irreversible surrender to God. Complete transference of ownership.

It's the master key to holiness, which leads to divine encounters and power.

It's a disconnection of anything that would contaminate a relationship with a perfect God.

It's complete surrender to allow God to possess us with Himself.

It's the open door to the divine riches and fullness of salvation & redemption.

It's a dying to the purposes and plans of self and a rebirth into the purposes and plans of God.

It's our consent and permission to God to allow Him to work in and through us.

It's the mandate for the manifestation of the promises of God.

"Consecrate yourselves, for tomorrow the LORD will do amazing things among you'" (Joshua 3:5).

It's the gateway and path of divine direction and reveals the will of God for your life. Romans 12:2

It's the greatest gift to God that one can ever present.

How do we remain consecrated? One way we can live a lifestyle of consecration is by prayer and fasting. Constant dying to self and getting filled and empowered for His purposes and plans. Prayer and fasting are not a suggestion or an option for a born again believer. Jesus said in His Word "WHEN ye pray" and "WHEN ye fast." Not IF. (Matthew 6:5 and 6:16)

I remember so many times, where my husband and I would go up to the altar at our church in Tampa, in our home, in our vehicle, even on the grass field of a tent crusade - and cry out to God, consecrating ourselves saying the same consecration prayer! "Lord use me! I'll go where you want me to go, I'll do what you want me to do! I'll say what you want me to say. Not my will but Thine be done!"

It is vital that you remain consecrated and separated. When God can get you all alone and in the secret place with Him, that's when He can really speak to you. He wants your undivided attention. Notice, whenever Jesus went away to pray and fast, He had divine encounters with God. God will cover you with His glory and you will find yourself walking in a greater level of the gifts of the spirit and the anointing that you've so greatly desired. Kathryn Kuhlman said "I surrendered unto Him all there was of me; everything. Then for the first time I realized what it meant to have real power." Consecration = Power.

Everyone wants power but not everyone is willing to pay the price of consecration. Doing whatever it takes to die to the flesh and purify and sanctify yourself for His glory! Have you consecrated yourself before God? Why don't you join me right now in this same prayer of consecration:

> **"Lord use me! Make me a vessel unto honor for the Master's use! I consecrate myself before you, all for Your service and purpose. Make me, mold me. I'm Yours! I'll go where you want me to go, I'll do what you want me to do! I'll say what you want me to say. Not my will but Thine be done!"**

3. Get Full of Faith

There's no way you can take dominion without being full of faith. People can definitely be full of doubt, but I'm talking about being full of FAITH. I'm talking about being submerged in faith. Some of you need a fresh baptism of faith! You once were running and believing God for something with everything in you. At some point life got busy then you lost hope and put that thing on the altar. God wants to give you BIG THINGS! He didn't create you to dominate

> God wants to give you BIG THINGS!

the earth and then to just give up or to give in. Mankind is next in command on this earth to God Himself!

Acts 11:24 says that Barnabas was a *"good man, full of the Holy Ghost and full of faith"*. In Romans 4:20 it says of Abraham that, *"He staggered not at the promise of God through unbelief; but was strong in faith, giving glory to God."*

Hebrews 11:1 *"Now faith is the substance of things hoped for, the evidence of things not seen."* 11:6 *"But without faith it is impossible to please him: for he that cometh to God must believe that he is, and that he is a rewarder of them that diligently seek him."* Vs 15 says *"These all DIED in faith."* Are you so full of faith that you are willing to die for your faith and for what you believe? When you are full of faith, you can relentlessly pursue your purpose. Faith triumphs over fear, it cancels it out. Settle within you what you believe! Settle that you will stand for it, no matter any obstacle. Being full of faith overpowers anything else that would try to come in and contaminate. Remember, all things are possible with faith and that with faith you can move mountains!!

4. Press Into It!

The definition of press is: to move or cause to move into a position of contact with something by exerting continuous physical force. It also means: to apply pressure to something to flatten, shape or smooth it.

When we press into the things of God, things happen! We press through for our breakthrough, for our promise! There's a purpose for the pressing, and it's to experience a desired result. Philipians 3:14 says, *"I press toward the mark for the prize of the high calling of God in Christ Jesus."* The Amplified version says,

"I press on toward the goal to win the [heavenly] prize of the upward call of God in Christ Jesus.

Look at Matthew 7:13-14: *"Enter ye in at the strait gate: for wide is the gate, and broad is the way, that leadeth to destruction, and many there be which go in thereat: 14 Because strait is the gate, and narrow is the way, which leadeth unto life, and few there be that find it. Amplified version says, "Enter through the narrow gate. For wide is the gate and broad and easy to travel is the path that leads the way to destruction and eternal loss, and there are many who enter through it. But small is the gate and narrow and difficult to travel is the path that leads the way to [everlasting] life, and there are few who find it."*

Notice, the way through the narrow gate is restricted by PRESSURE.

Luke 16:16 *"The law and the prophets were until John: since that time the kingdom of God is preached, and every man presseth into it."*

Matthew 11:12 *"And from the days of John the Baptist until now the kingdom of God suffereth violence, and the violent take it by force."*

The Kingdom of God requires you to PRESS into it. You have to take by force the dominion and the rightful position that is due to you. It is rightfully yours. All you have to do is to occupy. Press to take it! Be relentless in your stance, strong in your faith, and don't back up because things don't seem easy. Trust your God and trust His Word. You have to get desperate. You've gotta be willing to just flat out push past everything and get to business! The Bible says *that faith without*

> Be relentless in your stance, strong in your faith, and don't back up because things don't seem easy.

works is dead (James 2:26). There's an action required once you believe. Faith has footsteps.

Look back at the story of the woman with the issue of blood that we talked about in Chapter 6 (in Mark 5). Remember, this woman pressed through the crowd to get to Jesus? She said, "If I may touch but His clothes, I will be whole." If she could only just get to the hem of His garment....the Gentile woman we talked about, she only wanted to get to the CRUMBS under the children's table! How desperate are you for your miracle to fulfill your purpose on the earth? You were called to be a WINNER!

When you press: impossibilities become possibilities, manifestations of the promise become fulfilled, destinies are unlocked, undeniable miracles begin to take place, and new doors began to open!!! Hallelujah! Rise up, oh daughter! Take your place! Be fruitful, multiply, fill the earth and subdue it! And take DOMINION! In Jesus' name! Selah

I would like the final workbook in this book to be on Goal Setting. I believe that we must put action into what we read. Otherwise, it's just information that can be forgotten or lost into history. God's Word is more than information. It is about a transformation in your body, soul, and spirit. Let's first talk about purpose. What are your passions, dreams, and innermost desires that motivate you the most?

_____

_____

_____

_____

_____

_____

_____

Now, seek God in prayer and in the next minutes or so, and write down some ideas on what you can do with those passions to further the kingdom of God. How can you use them to make a kingdom impact for souls?

_____

_____

_____

_____

_____

_____

Next, I want you to make a timely goal to reach this vision. And then, place steps into a weekly and daily time slot. If you fail to plan, you plan to lose. Bishop David Oyedepo said, "Planning is winning as breathing is living." Plan your work and work your plan. Planners are achievers!

_____

_____

_____

_____

_____

_____

_____

_____

I believe in you because God is with you and He is in you. And whatever He shows you, He will bring it to pass! When you do your part, He will do His. Taking dominion comes by means of action! And I believe you are a daughter of ACTION!

Goal #1 _____

_____

Goal #2 _____

_____

Goal #3 _____

_____

_____

Weekly Commitments to reach goals:

Sunday	Monday	Tuesday	Wednesday	Thursday	Friday	Saturday

This is just a start. Maybe you only have one goal right now that you believe you can commit to. Perhaps you have 5. Please feel free to type this out in whichever format works best for you, on another sheet of paper or in your Journal. Commitment is the biggest key. Be diligent and make time for your goal. You are in this to win! You have one shot at this life on earth. People are counting on you to help them. I believe you can take dominion and make a major kingdom impact for Jesus!

Epilogue

I pray that this book ministered to you and helped you to discover the significance in being born as a woman, and being born again into the family of God. As you can see, you were created for a purpose. A kingdom purpose. You were created to raise a standard in the world around you, in a world of chaos. Though the devil was against the seed of the woman, God saw it that Jesus was born so that He could bring redemption and power into His children to live victoriously and eternally with Him! God saw to it that you were born and that you continue to multiply seed that will bring forth fruit into this world. The devil cannot touch your seed because you are a daughter of dominion!

A daughter of dominion is set apart from women of this world. As she develops and grows spiritually, it is evident in her personal life and to those around her. Her character stands out and is a blessing to her husband, to her children, and to her world. She builds and doesn't tear down. She promotes and not demotes. She encourages people and doesn't discourage people to live holy and victorious. She is pure, holy, modest, strong, kind, and fears the Lord. She is submissive to and respectful to her husband because she wholeheartedly trusts God and His Word and promises to her for obedience and the blessing.

No matter what her background, past struggles or failures may have been she rises to the top and accepts God's everlasting

Covenant so that she can be adopted as a daughter. As a daughter you can claim and eternally own your rights to this kinship. He is the Kinsman Redeemer (your Husband) who has bought you back (His bride) and will return again to bring you into eternity with Him. You have all rights and privileges in His Covenant and everything in the Bible is for YOU, both Old and New Testament. Every promise of God stands, yesterday, today, and forever.

Because you are in His eternal Covenant, you have the power within you to take dominion! In Ephesians 3:20 we read: *Now unto HIm that is able to do exceedingly abundantly above all that we ask or think, according to the power that worketh in us.* This power comes by being his child! As a daughter, you rightfully have this power. Do not let the enemy take it from you! You have a job to do. Now, you must renew your mind with the Word of God daily. Write the vision and get those scriptures on some index cards and place them where you can see them regularly. And most importantly, get His Word into your heart, your spirit. Next, get consecrated. Draw a line in the sand and say "Lord, I'm hungry." "I'm hungry for more of you!" Don't get satisfied, don't settle for where you are or how things have always been. Fast and pray, make a prayer of consecration between you and God and place yourself on the altar. Be willing to give up or to give Him anything He asks for. Remember a seed does not bear fruit until it dies (see John 12 :24). Die to the flesh and everything you own and surrender it all to Jesus. After this, you need to get full of faith. Dare to believe God right at His Word and right at what He says to you. Stand strong, unwavering and be bold. Lastly, press into it. Get desperate. Be willing to press even when the pressure may hurt or be stretching. Look at the vineyard and how grape juice is made. By pressure the grapes are pressed down to produce that sweet and strong grape juice. The Bible says in Matthew 7:13-14: *wide is the gate that leads to destruction and many are on that path. It's the easy way. But narrow is the path that leads to eternal life and few there be that find it.* Now we'll Look again at this scripture. This time in AMPC:

"Enter through the narrow gate; for wide is the gate and spacious and broad is the way that leads away to destruction, and many are those who are entering through it. But the gate is narrow (contracted by pressure) and the way is straitened and compressed that leads away to life, and few are those who find it."

Read Deuteronomy 30:19 AMPC

"I call heaven and earth to witness this day against you that I have set before you life and death, the blessings and the curses; therefore choose life, that you and your descendants may live."

You have a choice daughter of God. And I thank God for your choice to choose life, the narrow gate, that you will not bow down due to pressure. But that you will press into His kingdom and stand strong and be a witness to a world that is so desperately needing you. You are blessed and you are a blessing! I pray that as you decide to take that narrow path to eternal life, you hear these words *"Well done thou good and faithful servant: thou hast been faithful over a few things, I will make thee ruler over many things: enter now thou into the JOY of the Lord!"* (Matthew 25:21)

As a daughter of the King, you are a servant, a representative, and an ambassador to His glorious everlasting kingdom!

Declare this over yourself!!!

I am:

Righteous

Holy

Redeemed

Forgiven

Unashamed

Set Apart

Victorious

Rich

Fruitful

Virtuous

Triumphant

Favored

Called

Appointed

Predestined

Loved by God

On Fire for God

I am an Ambassador for Christ

A Preacher of Good News

A Demonstrator of the Gospel

A Worker of Miracles

A Partaker of the Heavenly Calling

Made in the Image of God

Separated from my mother's womb

Ordained as a Prophet to the Nations

Fearfully and Wonderfully Made

A Daughter of the King

A Child of Promise

A Joyful Mother of Children

A Pillar of Faith

A Habitation of His Presence

Justified by Faith

Reconciled to God

Clothed with Strength and Dignity

I am the Sweet Fragrance of Christ

Eternally Focused

Spiritually Minded

A Champion

A Soulwinner

A Shining Light in the World

A Habitation of His Presence

A Chosen Vessel

A Living Sacrifice

Ingrafted in Christ Jesus

Seated in Heavenly Places

Sealed by the Holy Spirit

Blessed with all Spiritual Blessings

Kept by the Power of God

Healed by the Blood of Jesus

Overcome by the Blood of the Lamb and the Word of My Testimony

I am unstoppable

A Good Thing

Full of Faith

Full of Life

Full of love

The Seed of Abraham

Joint Heirs with Christ

Elected by Grace

Freed from Sin

Spiritually Minded

Washed by His Blood

Complete in Him

Undefeated

Born for Greatness

Steadfast, Unmovable, Always Abounding in the Work of the Lord

I am an End-Time Revivalist

The Standard God is Raising Up

The One That Will Turn the World Upside Down

I am…..a Daughter of Dominion!!!!

Salvation for You & Daily Confessions

The greatest miracle that can ever take place in your life is salvation in Jesus Christ. This is the only way to become a daughter of the King and the only way to heaven. He died on the cross for your sins, sickness, poverty, and lack. He died on the cross and rose from the dead, so that you can and eternal life with Him. When you receive salvation, you have eternal life in Him guaranteed. You are transferred from death to life and from darkness to light, from a destiny in hell to a destiny in heaven forever.

The name of Jesus is above anxiety, depression, fornication, fear, addiction, and bondage. He is here to set you free!

If you have never accepted Jesus as your Lord and Savior or if you are not sure of where you will spend eternity, you can have assurance today. It doesn't matter if your father is an Apostle or grandmother was a Prophetess. This is personal, just you and Jesus like the woman we read about, in John Chapter 8, when all her accusers walked away. It's time to get real with Jesus.

Maybe you were once saved, when you were a child or a teenager. But you know that there is sin in your life. Jesus said He wants you either cold or hot, on fire for Him. He said if you are lukewarm, He will spit you out of His mouth. That was my issue. I was saved and baptized as a young child in church. But as I shared earlier in this book, I strayed from God for many years. And I had to come back to the Cross and be real with Him and surrender my all for the first time in my life, as an adult. If you are living with lust and fornication, anger, jealousy, unforgiveness, or any sin - it's time to come clean with Jesus today! And let Him give you the power and victory to overcome. Today is your day and right now is the time! Do not put it off. Tomorrow is not promised and you don't know when your last day on this earth will be. Hell is a real place. It was not created for people, but for the devil and his fallen angels.

When you sincerely say this prayer, the greatest miracle takes place. Your sins are washed away and Jesus promised to remember them no more. Though they are as red as scarlet, He washes them white as snow. You can have a clean and a fresh start.

The Bible says that *all have sinned and come short of the glory of God* (Romans 3:23). It also says: *For the wages of sin is death, but the gift of God is eternal life through Jesus Christ our Lord* (Romans 6:23). The Bible says that *whosoever shall call upon the name of the Lord shall be saved* (Romans 10:13). And you, my friend, are a whosoever!

Say this prayer with your heart and lips out loud:

Dear Lord Jesus,

> **I invite You into my heart to be my Lord and Savior. Forgive me of my sin. I forgive everyone who has ever hurt me. Wash me, cleanse me, set me free. Jesus I believe that you died on the cross for me. I believe that You rose from the dead, and that You're coming back again for me. Right now, I make a bold confession to turn from my sin and to turn to Jesus and begin to live according to Your Word. I commit and surrender my life to You, to speak Your Word over my life and to tell others about Jesus. Fill me with the Holy Spirit and the fire of God. Let me never be the same again. Thank You for your eternal Covenant with me, now Your Daughter and an heir of your eternal promises.**

In Jesus' name,

Amen

Now that you said that prayer, all of your sins are forgiven. The Holy Spirit is your Helper and He will help you to live victoriously and to overcome every obstacle in life. You are now redeemed and a born-again, blood bought believer of Jesus Christ. His Covenant and everything in it is for you!

There are 5 key things that you need to began implementing as a born again child of God, all that are in His Word for every believer:

1. **Word of God** - You need to begin daily reading your Bible. The Bible is your roadmap and guide to the knowledge of God and of the kingdom. The Bible says, *"Thy word is a lamp unto my feet, and a light unto my path."*(Psalm 119:105). The Word is life, it is everything you need and it has everything you need in it to live a victorious and holy life. We are to meditate on it both day and night. (Psalm 1).

2. **Prayer** - 1 Thessalonians 5:17 clearly tells us to *"Pray without ceasing."* When we pray, we build up our faith and strengthen our spirits. Prayer is our direct communication to God. Our prayers make things happen. When the church prays, mountains move!

3. **Worship** - Psalms 150:6 says, *"Let everything that has breath, praise the Lord. Praise ye the Lord.* Look at Psalms 100:

   Make a joyful noise unto the Lord, all ye lands.

   Serve the Lord with gladness: come before his presence with singing.

   Know ye that the Lord he is God: it is he that hath made us, and not we ourselves; we are his people, and the sheep of his pasture.

   Enter into his gates with thanksgiving, and into his courts with praise: be thankful unto him, and bless his name.

For the Lord is good; his mercy is everlasting; and his truth endureth to all generations.

When you love God, you worship Him. He deserves all of the honor and all of the praise. We humble ourselves and reverence Him in adoration because of who He is.

4. **House of God** - Psalms 122:1 says, *"I was glad when they said unto me, Let us go into the house of the LORD."* It is a privilege and an honor to come to the house of God and worship HIm. This is where we fellowship with other believers and get sharpened and fed by our under-shepherd. Hebrews 10:25 says *"Not forsaking the assembling of ourselves together, as the manner of some is, but exhorting one another: and so much more, as you see the day approaching."* We even get to bring and pay our tithe in the house of God and take our part in God's Covenant with the tithe. He promises that *He will open the windows of heaven and pour us out a blessing we don't have room enough to receive,* and so much more. (Read Malachi 3:10-12).

5. **Soulwinning** - As a believer, we must win souls. Proverbs 11:30 says, " *The fruit of the righteous is a tree of life; and he that winneth souls is wise."* Jesus also gave us the Great Commission in all 4 Gospels, and the book of Acts. Mark 16:15 says, *"And he said unto them, Go ye into all the world, and preach the gospel to every creature."* (You will find a free Gospel Soulwinning Script in the back of this book that you can feel free to copy and use. You can also find this script and other soulwinning tools on revival. com. Stick with the script and don't change it. This is the script I used to personally lead 384 souls to the Lord in just one week!)

Confessions:

I once had a woman ask me, "Who are you?" I knew that I was a child of God. I gave a text book answer and it came from the heart and it was correct. However, I began to look into this and documented many places in the Word of God that defined who exactly I was as a child of God. Boldly declare these confessions over your life and as you do, you will be built up spiritually and increase in faith and power as a daughter of the Most High.

Who Am I?

» I am complete in Him who is the Head of all principality and power (Colossians 2:10)

» I am made in the image of God and appointed to the nations of the earth. (Genesis 1:27; Jeremiah 1:5)

» I have a mouth that is filled with His praise and honor all the day. (Psalm 71:8)

» I am alive with Christ (Ephesians 2:5)

» I have speech that is always gracious, seasoned with salt, and I know how to answer each person. (Colossians 4:6)

» I am speaking, as one who speaks oracles of God. (1 Peter 4:11)

» I am free from the law of sin and death. (Romans 8:2)

» I am far from oppression, and fear does not come near me. (Isaiah 54:10)

» I am born of God, and the evil one does not touch me. (1 John 5:18)

» I am holy and without blame before Him in love. (Ephesians 1:4; 1 Peter 1:16)

» I am God's child for I am born again of the incorruptible seed of the Word of God, which lives and abides forever. (1 Peter 1:23)

» I am God's workmanship, created in Christ unto good works. (Ephesians 2:10)

» I am a new creature in Christ. (2 Corinthians 5:17)

» I am a spirit being alive to God. (Romans 6:11)

» I am a believer, and the light of the Gospel shines in my mind. (2 Corinthians 4:4)

» I am a doer of the Word and blessed in my actions. (James 1:22, 25)

» I am a joint heir with Christ. (Romans 8:17)

» I am more than a conqueror through Him Who loves me. (Romans 8:37)

» I am an overcomer by the blood of the Lamb and the word of my testimony. (Revelation 12:11)

» I am a partaker of His divine nature. (2 Peter 1:3-4)

» I am an ambassador for Christ. (2 Corinthians 5:20)

» I am a chosen generation, a royal priesthood, a holy nation, a peculiar people, whom God hath taken out of darkness and into His marvelous light. (1 Peter 2:9)

» I am the righteousness of God in Jesus Christ. (2 Corinthians 5:21)

» I am the temple of the Holy Spirit; I am not my own. (1 Corinthians 6:19)

» I am the head and not the tail; I am above only and not beneath. (Deuteronomy 28:13)

» I am blessed in the city and blessed in the field. Blessed coming in and blessed going out. (Deuteronomy 28:3,6)

» I am rich and financially increasing daily as I seek and put first His kingdom. (Deuteronomy 28:2; Malachi 3:10-12; Matthew 6:33)

» I am His elect, full of mercy, kindness, humility, and long-suffering (Romans 8:33; Colossians 3:12)

» I am forgiven of all my sins and washed in the Blood. (Ephesians 1:7)

» I am delivered from the power of darkness and translated into God's kingdom. (Colossians 1:13)

» I am redeemed from the curse of sin, sickness, and poverty. (Deuteronomy 28: 15-68; Galatians 3:13)

» I am firmly rooted, built up, established in my faith and overflowing with gratitude (Colossians 2:7)

» I am called of God to be the voice of His praise. And I am a voice to my generation! (Psalm 66:8)

» I am healed by the stripes of Jesus. And any sickness that would even try to come near my body DIES in Jesus' name! (Isaiah 53:4-5; 1 Peter 2:24)

» I am raised up with Christ and seated in heavenly places. (Ephesians 2:6; Colossians 2:12)

» I am greatly loved by God. (Romans 1:7; Ephesians 2:4)

» I am strengthened with all might according to His glorious power. (Colossians 1:11)

» I am submitted to God, and the devil flees from me because I resist him in the name of Jesus! (James 4:7)

Here is the Gospel Soulwinning Script from revival.com. Feel free to use this as a tool for soulwinning. You can print more and get more information on evangelism and tools at: www.revival.com/soulwinning tools. It is copyrighted, so please copy it right.

THE GOSPEL
SOUL-WINNING
—SCRIPT—

Has anyone ever told you that God loves you and that He has a wonderful plan for your life? I have a real quick, but important question to ask you. If you were to die this very second, do you know for sure, beyond a shadow of a doubt, that you would go to Heaven? [If "Yes"— Great, why would you say "Yes"? (If they respond with anything but "I have Jesus in my heart" or something similar to that, PROCEED WITH SCRIPT) or "No" or "I hope so" PROCEED WITH SCRIPT.]

Let me quickly share with you what the Holy Bible reads. It reads "for all have sinned and come short of the glory of God" and "for the wages of sin is death, but the gift of God is eternal life through Jesus Christ our Lord". The Bible also reads, "For whosoever shall call upon the name of the Lord shall be saved". And you're a "whosoever" right? Of course you are; all of us are.

continued on reverse side—

I'm going to say a quick prayer for you. Lord, bless (FILL IN NAME) and his/her family with long and healthy lives. Jesus, make Yourself real to him/her and do a quick work in his/her heart. If (FILL IN NAME) has not received Jesus Christ as his/her Lord and Savior, I pray he/she will do so now.

(FILL IN NAME), if you would like to receive the gift that God has for you today, say this after me with your heart and lips out loud. Dear Lord Jesus, come into my heart. Forgive me of my sin. Wash me and cleanse me. Set me free. Jesus, thank You that You died for me. I believe that You are risen from the dead and that You're coming back again for me. Fill me with the Holy Spirit. Give me a passion for the lost, a hunger for the things of God and a holy boldness to preach the gospel of Jesus Christ. I'm saved; I'm born again, I'm forgiven and I'm on my way to Heaven because I have Jesus in my heart.

As a minister of the gospel of Jesus Christ, I tell you today that all of your sins are forgiven. Always remember to run to God and not from God because He loves you and has a great plan for your life.

[Invite them to your church and get follow up info: name, address, & phone number.]

Revival Ministries International
Please, register as a Soul Saving Station at revival.com/JoinS3 and log your soul count regularly.

Made in the USA
Middletown, DE
28 April 2023